YOUR SECOND TO LAST
CHAPTER

YOUR SECOND TO LAST
CHAPTER

Creating a Meaningful Life on Your Own Terms

PAUL WILKES

YOUR SECOND TO LAST CHAPTER
Creating a Meaningful Life on Your Own Terms
Paul Wilkes

Edited by Gregory F. A. Pierce
Cover design and typesetting by Patricia A. Lynch
Photos by Paul Wilkes

Copyright © 2015 by Paul Wilkes

Published by In Extenso Press
Distributed exclusively by ACTA Publications, 4848 N. Clark St.,
Chicago, IL 60640, (800) 397-2282, www.actapublications.com

Library of Congress Number: 2015955664
ISBN: 978-087946-565-0 (paperback)
ISBN: 978-087946-566-7 (hardcover)
Printed in the United States by Total Printing Systems
Year: 25 24 23 22 21 20 19 18 17 16 15
Printing: 10 9 8 7 6 5 4 3 2 First

♻ Text printed on 30% post-consumer recycled paper

CONTENTS

THE CHAPTERS OF OUR LIVES

A loyal and hard-working servant to the king was walking outside the palace walls and fell into a ravine. And there encountered a genie. The servant could have one wish and it would be granted without question. Anything. He thought for a moment, then said, "I have worked hard all my life, serving others. Now I wish to be served. I wish for everyone to obey my commands. And to do no more work."

"Your wish is granted," said the genie, and disappeared.

When the servant returned to the castle he was stunned to find his every wish immediately granted. For the first month, it was a paradise he had never known. In the second month, he grew restless, and after the third, he hurried to the ravine where the genie awaited him.

"Whatever I wanted was given to me. I needed do nothing at all. I served no one. I was served from the moment I arose to the moment I went to bed. In the beginning, I enjoyed my new life. But now I am in agony. My life had no meaning. You must take this wish back."

The genie turned to leave. "I cannot. I granted you one wish, and one wish only."

"But this is like living in hell!" the servant pleaded.

"Where do you think you have been for these ninety days?"

A Time Like No Other

We Americans find ourselves, for perhaps the first time in human history, in an economy when a significant number of women and men of average means — not only the wealthy — will live many years without having to work for a living. They will be without major responsibilities, without significant concern about material needs.

It was not always so, as those of us in what are euphemistically called the "retirement years" well know. In our parents' generation, a man or woman worked until age 65 or so, lived on Social Security and perhaps some small savings after that, hoped for a few years of reasonable health (men fewer years than women), and then departed this life.

With modern medicine and financial pension benefits that can range from the reasonably comfortable to the very comfortable, Americans today are the first generation to have twenty or even thirty extra years of what could be termed "productive life" remaining. It is an uncharted and unwritten chapter and many of us are unsure what voyage lies ahead, what its pages might someday read.

It is this chapter, what I am calling "The Second to Last Chapter," that I want to explore with you in this little book. So what are the "chapters" of our lives, overlapping as they might be?

First: At Home and Developing

At first completely dependent, we gradually develop independence and the ability to function outside the protective environment of the home. We form an idea of the world around us from a limited group of people, mainly our parents. We may be somewhat naïve, but we are idealistic, we dream great dreams, envisioning heroic paths for our life. No one understands us, and certainly not the secret yearnings of our souls.

Second: At School and Learning

The number of years vary, but we receive a formal education. We are partially or entirely free of parental influence. Other ideas and values are presented and we sift through and evaluate both those and our own as we are formed into a more independent individual. We question more, we sometimes fall into cynicism, seeing the foibles of human nature. We rebrand our youthful cynicism and call it discernment or intellectualizing. We take all this conflicting information and storms of our mind into our mature life. Our idealism is more interior as we become more aware of the sacrifices idealism requires, but it is still there, deep in our souls, in what we know to be the best part of who we are.

Third: Launching Career(s) and Striving

Our dependence and education are over and we must support ourselves. We may follow a well-charted path (practicing medicine would be good example), or we cast about for work we hope will be satisfying and provide us with what we desire materially. Many of us will have multiple or serial careers where we devote a large portion of our time and energy. Our work may excite and energize; at times it appears as no more than a means to an end. We continue to seek work that challenges us and uses our particular skills. The word "practical" has new meaning.

Fourth: Relationships, Marriage, and Raising Children

We find a mate, and, like a career, there may be more than one. We may or may not marry. We may or may not have children. We now must apportion time between career — in which we are now more experienced — and family or relationship responsibilities, whatever those might be. These are our most productive years; our energy is abundant, our hopes are continually high for interpersonal happiness and fulfilling work.

Fifth: Children Leave; Career Levels Off and Ends

Usually within the decade that our children leave home permanently and we are in our fifties to sixties, we find ourselves at the end of the career or careers we have pursued. We may be pleased or disappointed in what we have achieved. But there are fewer demands made of us; our material needs are likewise less and, within reason, met. We look ahead. What will it be, a life of relaxation, rest from our labors? Doing those things we never had time for? Could there be something else, as we realize that we could live many more years without the demands and structure of our life up to now?

Sixth: The Second to Last Chapter

We have time and maybe the resources to explore doing something we might have always wanted to do but never had the time or opportunity to try. This is the chapter this book will explore, "The Second to Last Chapter." It is the one that is least explored, partly because it is relatively new in human history — especially for men, many of whom used to go directly from their work lives to their "last" chapter. I call the people in this group the "SLCs."

Seventh: The Last Chapter

We age and, depending on our health, need assistance or are able to live independently. We do not have the energy we once had, but may still be in reasonably good health. Our activities lessen, our world becomes smaller, but these are not necessarily unpleasant years; there is a mellowness about them. We find ourselves looking back over our life. Did it turn out as I had hoped? Is there anything I would have changed? Did I become the person I knew, in my soul, I was meant to be?

Our Life, Simplified?

Of course, few lives fall into neat categories or chapters, but roughly, those seven chapters encapsulate what many of us will experience. A child with severe and ongoing medical problems, the need to care for grandchildren or aging parents, our own physical or mental health, career setbacks, troubled relationships may demand everything of us.

But, for many of us as we arrive at The Second to Last Chapter, we experience a time in our lives when we are more aware of our abilities, more in command of our resources and — most importantly — our time, than ever before. And we are free to...do what...be what?

That is why I felt I needed to write a whole book about it.

It is not that we haven't looked ahead to these years. We have considered the options and have seen people our age as they embark upon this life chapter. Some possibilities:

+ Being the ideal, on-call grandparent may be the "career" you have been yearning for. You know, little children to care for, to love, have fun with, yet being able to return them to their parents and go on with your own life.

+ It might be travel for which you never had the time or money, that hobby you always wanted to invest in full time, finally being able to put in a few hours of volunteering each week, or simply stepping back from full-time involvement in a business or profession that once took all your energy.

+ For some, it is the idealized life, relaxing and "Doing whatever I want whenever I want — or don't want — to do it."

But I will never forget that sobering day, when I was in my early sixties and approaching My Second to Last Chapter. I was driving on a street that skirted the edge of the local country club golf course. And there he was, a man about my age, perhaps a bit younger. He was dressed in a bright lime-green sweater and his slacks and shoes bespoke a man who only wore the best. He was coming off a green at midday and walking toward the next tee. I saw his sad face for a moment — a flash really, like a single movie frame — and I surely could have been wrong. My instincts as a reporter for over forty years are not always accurate.

But I saw a spectral face, that of a hollowed-out man. Maybe he had just missed a putt. Or maybe — because I too was afraid to face what I would do in the years ahead — I saw him as a sort of modern day version of Scrooge's Ghost of Christmas Yet to Come. If you recall *A Christmas Carol*, that ghost said nothing and Dickens wrote that, in turn, nothing of note would be said of Scrooge at his funeral. Such would be Scrooge's fate, as a life closed, one of revering ledgers and allowing dreams to go unfulfilled and love to be unrequited.

The Alternative?

Think back to when you first had the feeling sweep over you that nothing was impossible, the future was bursting with possibilities. Or that heart-stopping instant when you realized you couldn't live without the person in front of you and that person said the feeling was mutual. Or when you found a work that you wanted to give everything to. That moment of spiritual transcendence, when the connection between you and the Divine Reality was so profound you knew that all the promises were true: your mustard seed could produce a great tree, you could move a mountain. Nothing was impossible, The Force was indeed with you.

To be fully alive, with the excitement of a new, open-ended adventure: That is what The Second to Last Chapter offers us, in ways few of us ever imagined. I did not, and I will tell you about that in detail later in this book. But for now I will say it quite simply: I have come to understand that *The Second to Last Chapter — with the freedom and abilities we now possess — has the potential to provide for us the most exciting and fulfilling years yet. I am talking about deep spiritual fulfillment, a true giving of ourselves to something that really matters, something that might not be done unless we do it.*

Remembering

When we were young, we might have thought about going off to the Peace Corps or becoming a medical or religious missionary to suffering people. We might have dreamed about going into politics or becoming a famous activist for a cause. Whatever our gallant dream, we envisioned how much good we could do...if only...if only. If only given the chance. If only we didn't have to complete school or support a family. If only our kids weren't so young. If only we had the money, the time, the skills, the opportunity.

I remember reading *National Geographic* when I was a teenager and seeing people living in desperate poverty. I don't know where it came from but the thought kept coming back: Someday I want to — I have to — help those people.

Dale Smith, retired business executive

On a parallel track, we look back now on our lives then: What truly mattered? What satisfied us, made us the happiest, the most fulfilled? The job promotion? The bigger house or newer car? I think not. Our lives — we — are so much deeper and profound than that. We found our true identity, our soul, when we were asked and we gave the most of ourselves.

Let me put this another way. When we realize that our spiritual core — our soul — is the most accurate gauge of who we are and what truly and deeply satisfies us, we can no longer relate to ourselves as merely a compilation of personal needs and worldly goals. These are woefully inadequate; our soul yearns for so much more.

I believe that in The Second to Last Chapter of our lives — perhaps even more so than when we were younger — we no longer are creatures merely seeking pleasures, even merely seeking peace. Ah, peace — that oft-sought-after goal that never is awarded to those who think it can be obtained by sheer will and not by abandonment of will. In these years of our lives, something happens. In the most cosmic sense, we regress to an earlier, simpler self. We become innocent, childlike in a way. The layers of sophistication and reasoning not so much melt away as become compartmentalized to allow us to open up to a new kind of lucidity.

Meaning. Purpose. Those two words swirl around in our brains. We want — our soul urges us — to live for something that matters.

The Hunger for Meaning

If I might try to put into words what went through my own mind as I entered My Second to Last Chapter: "I have only so many more years to live on this planet. During at least some of those years, however many they may be, I want to give myself to something that truly matters. My basic needs are taken care of. In fact, I don't need any *thing*. What I do need is *something* that will give the rest of my life *meaning.*"

In my late fifties and early sixties, as I found myself reviewing my life, I saw that at so many points it had been brimming with meaning. My struggle to get an education, my military service, finding a mate, raising a family, succeeding (a continual struggle) as a writer. All had mattered enormously to me and all had called upon everything I had. But as I looked ahead, the excitement of a fresh challenge that would ask me one more time for my best effort…well, I didn't see it. What would make me want to bound out of bed in the morning? What would trouble my dreams at night? I had always had a goal, something that possessed me. Now I needed something new.

It was not that I was neurotic (no more than usual!) or nail-bitingly anxious about it. I could do a little writing and gardening in the years ahead, take some nice vacations with my wife, spend time with my two grown sons. But I knew that would not be enough for me. That man walking off the green at the country club kept reappearing in my mind.

I knew I would never be one of those extraordinary individuals with unlimited funds, energy, and skills who, by sheer wealth or influence, could do whatever he or she wanted to do. Bill and Melinda Gates, with their good hearts and billions of dollars, can and will virtually eradicate polio throughout the world. Most of us do not have that capacity. But I wanted to do *something* with meaning, *something* beyond my everyday life. I asked myself a few questions:

- Was there a yearning within me to do something that truly matters?

- Was I willing to make sacrifices to accomplish that thing?

- Was I able to reach beyond what I thought were my limits, especially at my age?

- Did I want to help make the world…or, more realistically, a tiny portion of it…a little better place?

Bring your answers to those questions...or your own questions...along, and let's continue an exploration of *Your* Second to Last Chapter.

> There is only one thing that is truly insufferable, and that is a life without meaning. There is nothing wrong with the search for happiness. But there is something great — meaning — which transfigures all. When you have meaning you are content, you belong.
>
> Sir Laurens van der Post, *Hasten Slowly*

As transitions take place…a fundamental and primal shift from ambition to meaning occurs. The shift often takes the form of abrupt, unexpected changes in our lives…. With this shift comes an initial restlessness, irritability, anxiety, or discontent with our current situation, and a deep questioning of the motivation surrounding our choices in career and relationships. Everything comes up for review. Previous desires and choices to attain status, power, money, fame, or strategic relationships lose meaning and become unsatisfying.

Angeles Arrien, *The Second Half of Life*

DON'T LOOK FOR IT. IT FINDS YOU.

The pilgrims lined the road leading to the residence of the Dalai Lama in Dharamsala, India. They had come from all over the world, some hollow-eyed from everything from drugs to fasting, others with that glazed, expectant gaze. The moment was at hand, they were sure. I asked the Dalai Lama about them as we sat down for an interview for my documentary on Thomas Merton, the Trappist monk, who had once visited him.

"They are seekers and they come here to hear a word that will change their life or set them in the direction they should take," the Dalai Lama answered, a look of compassionate understanding on his face. "I wish I could, but I have nothing to tell them. I have no answers, none. All is already inside. We have to understand a simple truth: Do not look for it. It will find you."

My Story: The Beginning at Least

Many years later, on a blazingly hot afternoon, in India yet again, "it" found me. Quite by accident...or, thinking back, perhaps not by accident at all. The year was 2006.

My wife Tracy and I were in middle of a trip of a lifetime, four weeks in India. As for where I was in my life at that point: I was sixty-seven years old, in good health, happily married, our two sons grown and on their own. I had a long list of published books, television documentaries, and a fancy title as a "visiting writer" at a local university in North Carolina. I was not seeking a new direction; the path I was on seemed just about right. I was not thinking about chapters in my life, certainly not My Second to Last Chapter.

We had come to the city of Kochi in South India and checked into still another well-appointed hotel. Our driver picked us up promptly at nine, after we had finished a sumptuous breakfast. In our air-conditioned car, he showed us the oldest synagogue in this part of the world, unique Chinese fishing nets, a vibrant merchants' quarter. He was a perfect gentleman and wanted nothing to spoil our visit to his city. He talked proudly of Kochi's rich past as a seaport and its prosperous present, with one of highest literacy rates in India. He said nothing about the poverty that was all about us, the crippled and maimed, children begging on the streets, shacks made of scraps of metal and frayed blue plastic.

It was two o'clock, we still had time left on his services; what would we like to see or do, he courteously requested. Where this came from I will never fully know: "I'm Catholic," I blurted out. "What is my Church doing to help these poor people? Especially the children?"

This man was a professional driver and guide. He was used to the inane and sometimes unanswerable questions of tourists. He hesitated before answering. "I could tell you. But if you don't mind, sir, I'll show you."

We drove down Mohandas Gandhi Road, turned off at Binny Road, a narrow lane in a poor neighborhood in the Palluruthy district that had once been a swamp. He stopped at the metal gates of Prathyasha Bhavan, which translates into "Home of Hope." The gates swung open and a gaggle of girls came running toward us, laughing, waving their hands in welcome. They were neatly dressed, clean, and apparently happy. The grounds were well-kept, the buildings painted. It was an orphanage. All seemed well.

We were offered a tour of the orphanage by one of the Catholic nuns; I would find out that they were Salesian Sisters of Don Bosco, an order I knew from my early education. They had founded a school here some thirty years before.

As we walked through the building, it was soon apparent my first impression was wrong. All was not well; this was a very poor place. The children were sleeping on the concrete floor of the school's assembly hall, simply because there was no other room for them. In the pantry were a few bags of rice and a mound of wizened vegetables. The sisters were a bit shy, but finally admitted that at times they had difficulty feeding the ever-growing number of children, seventy-five of them that day. They would not — could not — turn away any child in need. The orphanage was living on the threshold of mere survival. And yet, we were asked for nothing and offered tea and cookies in the nun's small refectory.

The stories of the girls were horrific. One had been sold into prostitution at the age of eight. Another, a beggar, witnessed her mother being run over and killed by a train as they ran from police near the rail station. A seven-year-old had been forced to bury her baby sister whom her mother had suffocated just because she was another female. The girls had been sold into virtual slavery, beaten by parents, raped by fathers…young lives so tragically scarred… and these were the girls I had just seen laughing and grabbing my hand and already calling me "uncle."

We came outside into the hot sun and I plunged my hand into my pocket. I was ready to donate everything I had: dollars, rupees, traveler's checks. Suddenly, there on the dusty playground with a rusted swing hanging forlornly by a single chain, I spied a tiny girl standing in the shadow of one of the nuns, Sister Sophy Joseph. The little girl, named Reena, was wearing sunglasses.

None of the other girls were wearing sunglasses, and I asked why this child was wearing them. Sister Sophy reached down and gently removed the sunglasses. The little girl looked up at me. One of Reena's eyes was perfect, bright, like a dark pool in the moonlight. The other eye was a swirling mass of dead, grey tissue, terribly scarred and dull.

Sister Sophy spoke softly, so the girl could not hear. Reena had been begging on the streets with her mother, who was mentally ill. They were separated in the downtown crowds. Reena was kidnapped by the "beggar mafia." They dragged her to their hideout. Holding her down, hand and foot, they repeatedly plunged a darning needle into her eye, virtually gouging out that eye. They had plans for her, not only to be a beggar, but a "better" beggar, more pitiful, to bring them even more money. This was years before the movie *Slumdog Millionaire* portrayed this kind of cruelty to children.

I couldn't believe what I had just heard. The heat of the day suddenly rose up like the gates of hell had been opened in front of me. I couldn't breathe. I looked down at this tiny child, horror on my face. Little Reena looked up at me. And then she returned my look of horror with the most beautiful, trusting smile I had ever seen in my life.

Reena, when I first met her in 2006,
with the smile that changed my life.

Something happened. I don't know exactly what. But I knew that the paltry pieces of paper I was pulling out of my pocket to give to Sister Sophy were not enough, not nearly enough. To pat Reena on the head and say "Have a nice day, honey?" What could be worse than such arrogance?

Forget about having a nice day.... What about the rest of Reena's life? What did it hold for her, and was there any way I might help her?

I realized that Home of Hope needed far more than what I had in my hand. I needed to do more than leave a donation behind, get back into my air-conditioned car, and go on with my comfortable air-conditioned life. But what? And, more importantly, how? I was a free-lance writer, sixty-seven years old, no longer a young man.

What was I, one person, going to do? The needs I saw all around me that day were so profound. Where could I even begin to help?

I did get back into that air-conditioned car, but I was haunted by what I had just experienced. The thought kept occurring: If not me, who?

> I wrote some checks to take care of YMCA camp and after-school programs for a little girl named Trinity who was referred to me by social services as a girl in need, terrible family situation. It soon dawned on me. And then? I had to try to reshape her entire life.
>
> Judy Girard, President emeritus of the Food and HGTV Networks, who is creating a single-sex academy for girls in poverty in Wilmington, North Carolina

Oddly enough, our next stop on our India trip was not a typical tourist destination but Kurisumala, an ashram of Trappist monks high in the mountains three hours from Kochi. As I attended mass the next morning and walked the lush green compound, a mental video kept replaying in my head. Reena's story. My shock. Her radiant and trusting smile. I had trouble sleeping; I couldn't get the little girl out of my mind. We only had a short time left before getting on a plane to continue our journey, but I knew I had to see Home of Hope again.

This time when I drove through the gates and the girls came running toward us, I had a feeling that I had come home. Home... to Home of Hope. Remember, I had only been here for less than an hour the first time. I looked into Reena's face once again, and once again that trusting, loving smile asked nothing of me and yet countenanced everything.

I found these words forming in mind, but I was neither bold enough nor sure enough to say them out loud: "Reena, somehow, some way, I want to — I am going to — make your future better than your horrible past."

The air-conditioned car awaited me once more, this time to take me to the airport. My comfortable life awaited me in a few days, when I would return to America.

And once more I stood on that dusty playground, Reena in Sister Sophy's shadow. With her was another nun, Sister Thresia, who had invited us in for tea on our first visit. I kept saying good-bye, but then not leaving. The car hummed in the background.

"I won't forget you," was all that I managed to finally mutter.

When I got back to the United States I began to tell my friends about meeting Reena and her trusting smile. I found myself relating the story over and over, to anyone who would listen. I could see that Reena's story made the same impact on them that it had on me. People were ready to help, but I didn't know what to ask for or what to do. My mind kept revisiting that concrete floor where the children slept each night on a thin straw mat. I would start there.

That Christmas, I sent out a letter to my friends, asking them to contribute for "A Bed for Reena." We would buy foam mattresses and coverlets so the girls could at least get off that hard concrete floor. I collected about $3,000. It was a start and, as it would turn out, a foolish one.

The mattresses were a terrible idea. There was no place to store them during the day. The space was too crowded and the floor too dirty to keep them clean. But my new work had begun and, energized by the heartfelt response from my friends, I pressed on.

I am a journalist and was working on my next book while teaching at the University of North Carolina at Wilmington. I had become eligible for Social Security and, when I looked at how much I was earning at the university, I realized that if I took my Social Security and quit my job, my income would be less, but manageably less. The great difference would be in my time. I knew I was at a point in my life with more years behind than before me. I began to acknowledge that there was only so much oil left in my well. How did I want to pump it? And where did I want to use it?

Reena's smile held the answer.

If you take a quick look at www.homesofhopeindia.org, you will see what has transpired since 2006. Our list of accomplishments provides a good picture of where we started and where we are today. With eventual generous support from individuals, corporations, foundations, and civic and religious groups all over the world, we not only built a new orphanage for Reena and her friends but many more homes for orphaned, abandoned, and neglected girls. Homes of Hope has provided language labs, computers, hundreds of thousands of books, medical supplies, wells, water purifiers, farm animals, diesel generators, and much more that met many, many other needs.

In a short period of time, Homes of Hope has made a profound difference in the lives of thousands of children and young women. And its future could not be brighter, as more people learn about our work and join in.

And just to think: It all started with a little girl's smile.

I'll tell you more about the development of Homes of Hope later, but this is enough for right now. Because this book is not about Homes of Hope. Homes of Hope is just one example of the kind of small, targeted, nimble nonprofit that an ordinary person, like me...or you...can begin. If you want to. In The Second to Last Chapter of your life.

I got my feet wet with some local community projects, then a matching grant in India to fund water purifiers. Then I heard about hospital that had been demolished during the civil war in Sierra Leone. I gulped. A whole hospital? Sure, my cancer slowed me down a bit, but it also focused me: This had to be done. And done now.

Dale Smith, retired business executive

But wait, perhaps when you hear the story of a dramatic turn in a person's life, like this one was in mine, you draw back and say, "Well, good for you. Nice story, neat and clear cut. But things like that never happen in my life."

Well, actually they do happen. And they will continue to happen, if you allow yourself to be open to them. We'll be talking about that in the pages to follow. And believe me, it never is neat and clear cut; it is messy and frustrating. You'll be absolutely confident and absolutely dejected within the same hour. But as I look back, with all its aggravations and the blind alleys I've gone down, there have been far, far more moments of pure "all-right-ness." Homes of Hope is one of the great adventures of my life, one that I never could have imagined in what I began to see as My Second to Last Chapter.

And now, let's turn the attention to you and Your Second to Last Chapter. What can these years hold for you? What to do about those urges to "make a difference," those rumblings deep within you that will not be quiet?

Beware: There is only one thing worse than saying to yourself, "I am going to find something meaningful to do with my life!" That kind of white-knuckled approach really doesn't give your inner self — your soul — a chance to help you discern what is right for you.

What is worse than that? *Not saying* to yourself the exact same words, "I am going to find something meaningful to do with my life." The tone of your voice is what matters, really. Your best self responds best to a voice at once gentle and sincere. You don't have to shout. You just have to mean what you are saying.

The difference, however, is not the words, or even how you say them to yourself, but rather how you go about putting those dozen words into action.

Let's go deeper and pause to hear other voices that will either dispose you to open yourself to "it" or will convince you that all this talk about meaning and purpose in The Second to Last Chapter of your life, quite frankly, doesn't apply to you.

THE VOICES TO HEAR

Let us say you are at the local "big box" retail store on a crowded Friday afternoon. A woman in a checkout lane is juggling three young children, meanwhile carefully watching the tally on the register. A look at her shopping cart clearly shows she is trying to make her limited funds go as far as she can. There are plenty of inexpensive staples, all the generic store brand: detergent, light bulbs, plastic wrap, and a box of juice glasses, one broken, from the mark-down bin. She hurriedly leafs through a sheaf of coupons, double checking. The total rings up. She digs into her wallet, then the change pocket, finally dredging the bottom of her purse. The people in line shuffle their feet. A throat clears with impatience.

She doesn't have enough. She is embarrassed.

The young clerk worriedly looks down the line of customers, then to the counter. The three dollars that stood between what the woman had and the bill's total have been quietly placed there by someone. The clerk realizes what has happened. "Ma'am, I didn't count it right; here's your change. Thanks for shopping with us."

It's not important where the three dollars came from. More important is why? What motivated one individual in line — and no one else — to come forward to help a total stranger?

I think if we looked into the life of the generous person, we would find that this small but timely gift came from someone who had seen similar acts growing up, either by parents or people who made a lasting impact on them. A voice from the past whispered: "Get that three bucks out there. And be quick about it. And don't let anybody notice."

Those voices, audible and inaudible, are replayed in all the chapters of our lives, forming the habits we practice, shaping the way we live our daily lives. And only after we have acted do we realize what voice we heard. It was a natural response of the person who surreptitiously gave the three dollars to do the right thing and meet the immediate need. Simply put, his or her voices "made" him or her do it.

And the other people in line? They heard other voices. "Don't get involved." "She's probably on welfare." "Some people!" "I'm late; would somebody take care of this?" "Where's the manager?"

My Voices

Let me tell you about some of the voices in my own life. It is not even that I try to listen to them; I don't have much of a choice. As we will discuss later about what I call "Selfish Selflessness," I just feel more aligned, more myself, when I do. I am sure those voices were there, whispering so, so softly on that hot afternoon in India when I first met Reena.

I also want to offer you a chance to let your mind wander and hear voices from your past as you contemplate what Your Second to Last Chapter might hold.

And then let's talk about our other voices, the kind that often drive us inward to our own needs and comfort instead of outward to a world — or a person short three dollars — in need of what we can offer.

You see, we all have a choice of which choir of voices to hear.

But if you live for external achievement, years pass and the deepest parts of you go unexplored and unstructured. You lack a moral vocabulary. It is easy to slip into a self-satisfied moral mediocrity. You grade yourself on a forgiving curve. You figure as long as you are not obviously hurting anybody and people seem to like you, you must be O.K. But you live with an unconscious boredom, separated from the deepest meaning of life and the highest moral joys. Gradually, a humiliating gap opens between your actual self and your desired self, between you and those incandescent souls you sometimes meet.

David Brooks, *The Road to Character*

At Home

Mine was an archetypical second generation immigrant home, with more kids than beds, a blue-collar father, and plenty of hand-me-down clothes.

We were Slovaks, two parents and seven children, living on the East Side of Cleveland. My father, who had once worked in the Pennsylvania coal mines, was now a union carpenter. My mother not only raised us, but (and how did she do this?) cleaned houses for the rich ladies in Shaker Heights by day and in the evening worked at a dry cleaning factory. We were always aware that money was short and we couldn't waste anything. We ate plenty of potatoes (with tomatoes on top, it was billed as "ice cream"), and every Friday night it was corn meal mush with browned butter. We never thought of ourselves as poor, but we were.

And yet I remember Sunday mornings after Mass, when a good part of the neighborhood passed through the Wilkes kitchen for a bowl of my mother's delicious chicken soup and her homemade noodles. Or, Mom passing the plate of hamburgers around the crowded table for seconds, even before she had a first. "I ate at the stove while I was cooking," she would lie.

There were lessons I learned from the barroom as well as the kitchen during those Cleveland days. My father had perhaps the worst kind of carpentry work, rehabilitating commercial buildings after a fire. He would eventually die from black lung disease, both from inhaling ashen timbers and working in the mines. Each night after work, he would stop at Tom's Café on the corner of our street for a shot (or two) of a cheap whiskey and a glass (or two) of beer. "To clear my throat," he would say.

I must have been eight or nine when I was allowed to meet him at the tavern one afternoon, and I'll never forget him and his friends walking into the smoke-filled bar. While the others held back, chatting it up, my father reached into his pocket and pulled out a five dollar bill. He would buy the first round.

I saw him do this over and over as I grew up. Dad was always the first to offer to pay, even if it is was all he had. He bought dozens of eggs from a relative who had a flock of chickens, and then he gave away most of them. He also knew what kind of wild mushrooms were good to eat, and he would harvest baskets full of them from the woods and give away far more than he kept.

I look back now, in sadness. I was the only child in our family to go to college, and when I arrived on campus at Marquette University and other students said their father was "in sales" or "in banking," suddenly my carpenter father was "in construction." I grew ashamed of my humble beginnings, the smell of cabbage, honest perspiration, and threadbare winter coats.

But what my mother and father taught me, never so much as uttering a word, was more important than all the theology courses I took from the Jesuits: There is always enough, more than enough, to go around. You won't have less; you'll have more. Share it, give it away. Somehow, everybody will have what they need. (Come to think about it, that *is* what the Jesuits taught in their theology courses!)

In everyone's life, at some time, our inner fire goes out. It is then burst into flame by an encounter with another human being. We should all be thankful for those people who rekindle the inner spirit.

Albert Schweitzer

In Midlife

In my mid-thirties, my first marriage on the rocks, I turned away from my life as a rising New York writer and committed myself to life with the poor. I had met Dorothy Day, spent time at the Catholic Worker house on the Lower East Side, and decided I needed to strip away anything comfortable or easy. I left behind the expense account lunches and Brooks Brothers shirts. I became aggressively poor.

I wore ragged clothes with a haggard look on my face; ah, the martyr! I determined that I would live this saintly existence, unencumbered by any earthly need. Through the Worker, I found that Jacques Travers, a French professor, had a small house of hospitality and had taken in three homeless men. He took in another. Me.

I tried, tried so hard, but nothing lined up for me. I was revolted by Freddie, our ex-seaman cook, who wiped his face on the dish towel and then dried the dishes. Donald, a Vietnam veteran with post-traumatic stress syndrome, drove me wild, pacing our short hallway, still on sentry duty in the Mekong Delta. "The Professor," aged and immobile, lived in a Barcalounger, refusing to take to a bed, as he was sure he would die if he did. He would cache pieces of food within the recesses of his hallowed chair, afraid no more meals were forthcoming. Rats and cockroaches heartily approved of his pantry of ready treats.

And there was Jacques, so kind to them all, gentle, ready to hear their ranting and complaints. And there was me, Paul Wilkes, the voluntarily poor ex-writer, simmering at their ingratitude.

One afternoon Jacques and I were at the supermarket, much like the woman in the example above, trying to make our combined funds stretch for the week's food. We stopped at the wine display. After all, he was French, what was a meal without a glass of wine? I reached for Franzia, the cheapest brand, in a newly conceived way of packaging, a box. I put it in the cart.

"Oh, Paul, *mon cherie*, we must have a fine wine for our simple meals, it will bring out the," he hesitated to make sure he had the exact word, "…the bouquet," with "quet" accented. He reached for a new Beaujolais, a bottle costing twice as much as the box, yet yielding only a quarter as much.

Jacques, Jacques, you could never be poor, although you lived in a wretched Brooklyn apartment. Your *joie de vivre* could not be contained by something as banal as money.

In My Writing Life

Once I realized I was not destined to be a saint or martyr, I came back to my writing life. On my first story for *The New Yorker* magazine, I profiled Father Joseph Greer in Natick, Massachusetts.

The story was to show the daily life of a parish priest, his struggles and triumphs, and — as I was to find out with Father Greer — his unaffected, totally appealing humanity. It was at a time when people knew little about what a priest was like outside of his official functions and when the shortage of priests was placing an ever larger burden on the men who stayed in the cloth. Yes, I gave the needed statistics and made sure that his black suits were more wool than polyester (the famous fact-checkers at *The New Yorker* would not have it any other way), but I also followed Father Greer for many days, from morning mass to his nightly Manhattan cocktails.

I followed him as he trudged up the stairs at a shabby walk-up to console a newly-widowed and very cranky lady nobody else wanted to visit. He got a kid into Boston College who had a great heart but lousy grades. He sat patiently with a yuppie couple more focused on flower arrangements than the actual meaning of their upcoming marriage.

In his droll, unaffected way, Father Greer took on whatever problem or person that day presented. He was so matter-of-fact and undogmatic that at first it seemed little was happening in his ministry. But that was the beauty of the man. He derived a terrific kick out of helping people put the pieces of their lives together, finding a way over, through, or under whatever temporary barrier seemed to appear.

And when they offered him thanks or praise, he brushed it off. He had done nothing at all; what were they talking about? He was just passing by the widow's; he hadn't made a special trip. His call to the admissions officer at Boston College (who happened to be a classmate) meant nothing; what influence did he have? The couple had discovered the splendor and power of the wedding mass and ceremony on their own; he had just asked them a couple of simple questions.

So, among my choir of voices (and there are many, many more), each offering a different tone and message, are these three:

- The voice of my parents: Go ahead, give it away, share what you have and then some; there's always more coming.

- Jacques' voice: Never live life on the cheap; live luxuriously. Even as you eat humbly, make sure you wash it down with a good wine.

- Father Greer's voice: Step off the stage if there's applause; don't bask in the limelight. You know what happened; you don't have let everyone else know you know. You've already got your reward; now move on.

I teach them how to navigate life.

Poverty is a state of mind I wanted to change.

Gloria Carter Dickerson, one of thirteen children of sharecroppers, who founded *We2Gether Creating Change* to transform children's lives

Your Own Voices

As you read about three of the voices that continue to influence my life, I am sure you thought of your own voices.

Just sit for a moment and go through your life. Home life, school life, married life, working life. Good times, bad times. Best friends, teachers, girlfriends, boyfriends, spouses, children, siblings, parents, co-workers, priests, ministers, rabbis, imams, relatives, strangers. Books you've read, movies you've seen.

Fascinating isn't it, this search for voices? The vast majority of the people you have known for a lifetime won't be named to your choir. Yet there are others that you might have known for a short time, met only once, or actually never met at all, whose voices come calling across the decades to be remembered and given their place.

> For there are people one meets — in books and in life — with whom a deep resonance is at once established.
>
> Thomas Merton

What was it about those voices; why do you remember them? Some were incidental. Few, if any, were famous or known to other people as influential. Yet they resonated with you. And they come back to you often. At times theirs is an insistent voice, at other times it is quiet, gentle, surprising because it is so mysterious: Where did *that* come from? Why did I *think* that? Why did I *do* that?

Summoning or Recalling Those Voices

Allow me to suggest a simple way to welcome again the voices that echo in your soul as you approach Your Second to Last Chapter. Among the cacophony of voices you have heard over a lifetime, there were a few that were different from the rest. It was almost as if your voice and those voices somehow recognized in each other a commonality, a mutual understanding that made complete, unadulterated sense. You were able to utter "yes" as that voice inventoried not only who you are but also what you had inside you at that point in your life. Now, as you look to Your Second to Last Chapter, what you are reflecting upon is what you truly *could* be, from here on out. How can you live these years being what your inner voices want you to be: not out of guilt, but out of your own desire. Your voices have made a profound impact on you your entire life, listen to them one more time.

Below you will find a list of virtues to think about, with a short explanation of each. As you do, I would ask two things:

First, who comes to your mind as you read through the list? It isn't necessary to struggle to find someone for each virtue. You may pass over certain virtues that do not resonate with you, but many people may appear in your mind for other virtues. They can be real people or people you met on the pages of a book or saw in a play or read about in a newspaper. Friends you had as a child; people you just met yesterday. Let your mind wander, let your eyes move randomly over the list. If no one immediately comes to mind, don't worry. Your subconscious is a rich and cluttered storehouse. Open the door and let the dust fly out and fresh air fly in.

Second, reflect on what these voices might be saying to you at this point in your life. If you were to sit down and talk with them and tell them where your life is right now — and, perhaps, about your yet unfocused desire to do something significant with your remaining productive years — how might that conversation go?

Here is the list of virtues:

Compassionate: Someone who really "got it" about other people, who could see the good in everybody and was the last to judge. But then this person always went further and did what she or he could to make life better for others.

Courageous: Being tough on the outside; that's easy. This person had real backbone and stood up for what was right, whether it was popular or not.

Creative: The person who was excited by the power of ideas and inspired you to think outside the box. Maybe this person was a dreamer, but they were always great dreams, and he or she knew how to make some of them come true.

Discerning: This virtue goes beyond smarts or intelligence; it is about wisdom and intuition. This person could weigh all the facts, hear all the points of view, and come up with a clear-thinking approach or answer.

Enthusiastic: What was it about this person's joy? It was infectious. Positive energy and plenty of it. It was natural, not a mask. He or she was genuinely excited about life.

Generous: This person not only gave willingly and often, but did it in a natural way, often anonymously, and never asked for something in return.

Holy: Something about this person was sacred (although not necessarily pious). He or she may never have uttered a word about religion or morals, but there was something else, something that transcended everyday life, something you couldn't quite put your finger on, that was there.

Idealistic: This person truly stood out. You could always count on her or him to have the highest values…but it didn't stop there. She or he always acted on what was right or needed to be done.

Persevering: This person simply wouldn't take no for an answer. As you look back, he or she could stay the course no matter how long it took or how hard it was.

Trustworthy: In season and out, you could depend on this person. You might not have seen her or him for decades, but you knew if you called in the middle of the night, it was not in vain. If a promise was made, it was set in stone.

Another Voice

And there is still another voice, in your choir and in mine: our own voice.

It is often a little voice, often *sotto voce*, yet ever present. It is the murmuring of our own soul, the deepest, most authentic voice we have. It may seem that we have silenced it, or we have at least tried. There have been — and are — those times in our lives when we want to hear nothing from this voice; we want to will our way, regardless of anything or anyone. And we are successful. For a time.

Do not wish to be anything but what you are. And try to be that perfectly.
St. Francis de Sales

But our voice can never be silenced entirely, because it is in our very makeup, more true and telling than our DNA. What it sounds like and how we respond to it have been influenced by our upbringing and the influences that life has afforded. But it wants to be heard, because that voice charts the very pathway both inward, into the deepest and best part of ourselves, and outward, into a new world of openness and opportunity that awaits us.

I believe that The Second to Last Chapter in life offers a chance to reclaim that voice within. It is only that, an offer. I remember during my years of psychoanalysis learning about "the tyranny of the should," a concept of the psychiatrist Karen Horney, and realizing the hazards of my piling on "shoulds" in my own life. So I am the last person to use that word now. Listening to your own voice is not mandatory; you will not die if you do not listen to it, but I believe something inside you will become more alive if you do.

That "something inside you" is called by many names, but it holds the very secret to our well-being, our true and deepest happiness. For this is the realm of the *anima* or *animus* — where the word "animate" has its roots. It is here that our unconscious self constantly sends messages, signals, little flashes of insight, all demanding to be heard. It is our soul, the ground of our being, God, enlightenment — whatever name you want to give it — which understands us better than we understand ourselves and constantly seeks what is best for us.

Our voice is deeper than religious belief or any spiritual path. It is as unconscious as the breath we take in and release, without ever noticing. It is the very foundation upon which we might build, the beacon by which we might steer. If we listen for that inner voice, we will have a companion for The Second to Last Chapter like no other.

We cannot summon this voice. We can only welcome it by giving it the room to enter our lives and then listening to what it is saying to us.

The world is moving so fast these days that the man who says it can't be done is generally interrupted by someone doing it.

Harry Emerson Fosdick, Protestant minister

THE WRONG VOICES TO HEAR

You've just turned the page and — hmmm — perhaps, just perhaps, feel that little tingling within. That means you are still with me. You may be thinking:

- Yes, I've had those people who inspired me, people I wanted to be like.

- Yes, I can hear those voices.

- Yes, something inside me is urging me on to do more with my life.

But there are other voices demanding to be heard, other voices you will need to answer.

Beware of False Voices

Now that you've begun to think about what Your Second to Last Chapter might hold, let us listen to some other voices. I have heard them, you will hear them.

These voices will try to convince you that what you are wrestling with is foolish, wrong, untimely, futile, or all of the above. We all have heard these voices throughout our lives. They are the voices of "no," the voices that can shrivel our spirit and suffocate our soul — but we must answer them if we are to find the path that is best for each of us. Here is what they might say.

"Why do you want to get involved in something like this? You'll have more headaches and problems than you bargained for."

Actually, the voices are correct on one level. If you really try to do something that matters in Your Second to Last Chapter, there will be headaches ahead, plenty of them. Your best intentions may turn to dust. You will wonder, maybe often, why you ever started down this path in the first place. Here are some of my more magnificent failures:

+ I found that the bubblers on the new water purification system I had so carefully selected and purchased for our first orphanage building were 1) terribly overpriced; even though I told the shopkeeper where they were going, he still charged me triple and 2) terribly wrong; the water pressure was so strong that the stream almost knocked the girls over.

- I bought mattresses for the orphanage they couldn't use because there was no place to store them during the day, they got filthy on the floor, and they were too hot in the Indian summer.

- I purchased a Rosetta Stone program to teach the girls English and returned to find it gathering dust because no one knew how to use it.

- I sent a shipment of books by sea, only to have them impounded at the docks for almost a year and a huge customs fee had to be paid.

- I helped start businesses through microloans that failed miserably.

It took a couple years, but only after I developed a sense of humor about functioning in India and adopted a mantra did I begin to work, if not always successfully, at least a bit more peacefully. The mantra? Not so holy or profound or even original. Simply: "No good deed goes unpunished."

Because sometimes it seems that way, that no matter how well you plan, how many people you contact, how many Google searches you've done, you will get a stick in the eye for all your good intentions.

But then, on the other side of the ledger, we witness something else. With Homes of Hope, it was the smile of a ten-year-old girl sleeping on a bed for the first time; the tiny hand of an eight-year-old who had been cruelly raped and abused since she was an infant, taking mine as we walk the hallways of her new home; the pressed uniform and excellent hairdo on a nineteen-year-old, abandoned by her family, now in training at a major airline.

For me, the failures, the problems, fade away when I see what has been accomplished for these girls. Yes, it is all worth it. Whatever you decide to do with Your Second to Last Chapter will be worth it for you.

"You've never done anything like this before; isn't this a bit late to get started?"

Most likely you have never taken on a problem like hunger in your city, or seniors without transportation to the hospital, or girls living on the street in India. Well, what about it? We'll get to the "is this the right time of your life?" question in a bit.

All I can say, from my experience, is that if you put one foot in front of the other, see what other people are doing and learn from them, acknowledge and learn from your mistakes and build on your successes, you can do "it," whatever your "it" is. Because of the expertise you have developed in other parts of your life, plus talents yet untapped that you don't even know you have and the passion that will rise up within you to make a difference, you are more ready than you might imagine.

Look, I spent my life as a freelance writer, never balanced a checkbook, never took a management course, and knew nothing about organizational structures. But I did know how to ask a question and listen for an answer. I had learned how not to take "no" for a final answer. And I was experienced in moving from project to project (books, magazine articles, television documentaries), working hard on those that were jelling and leaving others to mature or quietly fade away. I have used all those skills to help Homes of Hope.

And, although Homes of Hope is a registered 501c3 nonprofit, I am working under the guidance of a group of brave, talented, and competent Catholic nuns in India who actually run the orphanages we build and the schools and hostels we support. I cannot tell you how many people I meet who go to India and, seeing all the children on the streets, immediately want to help found an orphanage. "No, no, and no," I tell them. "You do not want to found or run an orphanage in India. There are plenty of good groups in India that have the capacity to do that. What they lack is funds. If you want to help those kids, raise some money and give it to them."

When new aspects of our self emerge at different points in our life's journey, growth…requires that they be recognized and given their rightful place…. This dissolution provokes anxiety because it changes our sense of who we are…. The old self has to die for a new self to be born.

Wilkie and Noreen Cannon Au, *The Discerning Heart*

Just about every work you might take on to help make this world a better place will start out small. That is good. There's not too much damage you can do! You will stumble along at first, learning as you go, growing as you need to grow. My business school friends will probably stop reading right here, but you really don't have to have a five-year strategic plan. You will figure out what you should be doing as you go along. As you grow in Your Second to Last Chapter, your own abilities will grow and, more importantly, you will find other people to help you. You may not have an accounting degree or an engineering background, but someone out there does...and if what you are doing has appeal and meaning, they'll want to be part of it. You will also discover that other people have gone before you in pursuing your particular dream, and they will show you the way. You do not have to reinvent the wheel. Most of the time you just need to help grease the axle.

As for this being "the right time of your life," well...if not now, when? You certainly cannot rewind your life and do it all over again, and who knows what the future holds (except that we do know The Final Chapter will come in its own time). But realize that the statistics are on your side for doing something important now. The Second to Last Chapter years are a prime time to make a difference in the world. Providing your health holds up reasonably well and you can live within your means and there isn't a pressing issue (for instance, an aging parent or ill child that needs your constant care), if you are sixty years old you could easily have ten to twenty or even thirty years to make that difference. Providing, of course, you start now.

"Why get involved? And why does it have to be you?"

Let's turn this question around. Why *not* you?

In the compelling movie *The Imitation Game*, a mathematical genius, Alan Turing, is portrayed as difficult, distant, eccentric, and generally odd. He doesn't get along with a team that has a crucial task before them: to break the message code Nazis are using during World War II. At first, it appears Turing will never be asked to work on this important project; later, he is about to be fired. It appears that his abilities to crack code will never be put to use. There is a haunting line from the film that speaks to us as we think about these two opposing questions: why you/why not you?

Sometimes it is the people whom no one imagines anything of…
…who do the things that no one can imagine.

I will not even entertain the thought that you are not one of the people who want to make a difference in the world. You *are* one of those people. My evidence? You wouldn't be reading this far into this book if there wasn't something inside of you that will be not quieted, a feeling that keeps bubbling up when you least expect it. You know there is something out there for you to do in Your Second to Last Chapter.

What is it? That is the real question.

The biggest risk is that a lot of people will try to talk you out of pursuing your dreams. The world has too many people who are happy to discuss why something might not work, and too few who will cheer you on and say, "I'm there for you." The more time you spend navel-gazing, the longer you give those negative gravitational forces to keep you in their tether.

John Wood, founder of Room to Read, which has established thousands of free libraries throughout the world

Within each of us is a vast array of talents and abilities, only a fraction of which we ever get to fully utilize in our lives. Just as I have fantasized about going to medical school and serving in some remote area of the world, *a lá* Albert Schweitzer, I have also dreamed about being a hermit and living in a cave somewhere and writing soaring books of deep spirituality.

As for medical school, at my age and with my solid C's in chemistry and biology, I don't think they are waiting for my application. The hermit life? I actually tried it and found myself lonesome and miserable. Now, after more than thirty years of married life, I find myself in the right cave, with the right cave mate. Yet I still want to do something, and my "something," my "it," is Homes of Hope. The question hovers, tantalizingly appealing: What is your "it"? The answer is reassuring and simple: If you open yourself to the possibility, "it" will find you.

Certain paths will not be open to you. But dreaming great dreams and discovering a driving purpose in your life at your age are not only possible but surprisingly near at hand. You have probably been involved in causes and volunteer organizations before in your life. I'm sure at one time or another you said: "Why don't they just see the potential that's in front of them?" That is the beauty of the opportunity you have, now, to forge something that will tap the untapped resources within you and give you the opportunity to help shape a work that is important. Will you run into the same problems every other person who wants to make a difference in the world runs into? Most certainly.

But here is the reality: The work you will find to do in Your Second to Last Chapter might never have been done without you.

"It's hopeless; it'll break your heart."

In short:

+ When you really dig deep into the need you are trying to address, it *will* overwhelm you. And when you see what you *cannot* do, it *will* break your heart, again and again.

+ Hopeless? How many times in your life were you in "hopeless" situations that somehow turned around, yielding a great result? Besides, at your age, what have you really got to lose? Prestige? Status? Promotions? All are mistily in the rear view mirror.

+ Dietrich Bonhoeffer said we should be aware of "cheap grace." Regardless of how others assess you or your situation, *you* know what's burning inside of you. You need to do this for *you*, even if you may not succeed completely.

**"I accomplished a lot through my own efforts;
I earned this time in my life to rest."**

In short:

+ Really? Did everything by yourself, did you?

+ How much rest do you really need? (I never knew a hammock that was good for more than an hour.)

+ If you believe in a life after death, you'll have an eternity to rest. If you don't believe in a life after death, then all the more reason to get something done now!

"There are plenty of problems right in my community
Why should I run around looking for more?"

All I can say is that you fall in love when you fall in love. When we traveled to India, my wife, Tracy, was the executive director of a terrific organization called DREAMS of Wilmington, North Carolina (www.dreamswilmington.org). Through its programs of hands-on exposure to the arts, DREAMS shaped kids from the poorest neighborhoods into confident community leaders and sent the vast majority on to higher education or the military, prepared to take on life's challenges. I supported Tracy, helped in renovations, did whatever was needed, and went to every DREAMS function. Looking in from the outside, one might think I should have simply chosen to help Tracy raise money and awareness for DREAMS as My Second to Last Chapter, but the reality was that I had not fallen in love with DREAMS. Tracy understood this. I fell in love with the idea of making Reena's future better than her horrible past. I fell in love with that gaggle of girls that ran to the gate to greet me at Home of Hope in Kochi, India. They found me.

There is a danger in the "there are plenty of problems" thinking. If we can convince ourselves that there are an insurmountable number of horrors or needs wherever, we can rationalize our way into doing nothing about any of them. And what does that add up to? You got it. Nothing.

To be fully invested in a meaningful work, you have to fall in love with what you hope to do. You need passion, because you will be tested over and over again. So never feel you "should" or "have to" embark on a work only because there is a critical need. There are millions of critical needs. We can (and should) chose one on our own terms. That is why we each have an "it," and "it" will find us.

For we carry our fate with us — and it carries us.
Marcus Aurelius

So why try to fit into some stereotype of what Your Second to Last Chapter should be, why listen to negative voices as they try to drain the very energy you feel rising in you? You may even hear discouraging words from people who themselves are struggling to find a satisfying path for Their Second to Last Chapter. It may come from jealousy that you are so enthused, but more often it is regret on their part. They are trying to talk themselves out of the recurring feeling that *they* should be doing more by discouraging *you* from doing so.

Don't listen to any of these voices. Listen to the one that comes from deep within you.

SELFISH SELFLESSNESS

David Brooks, in his New York Times *column, took on "The Limits of Empathy," and his thoughts are worth mulling over. "Nobody is against empathy…. Nonetheless, it's insufficient…a way to experience delicious moral emotions without confronting the weaknesses in our nature that prevent us from actually acting upon them…. Empathy orients you toward moral action, but it doesn't help much when that action comes at a personal cost…. People who actually perform prosocial action don't only feel for those who are suffering, they feel compelled to act by a sense of duty. Their lives are structured by sacred codes."*

And the code these people live by, Brooks maintains, "…isn't just a set of rules. It's a source of identity. It's pursued with joy."

That's exactly what will motivate and sustain you in Your Second to Last Chapter. The seed of a feeling that something isn't right will begin to take root, blossoming into the determination to actually do something about it, not with grim determination, but naturally, organically, happily. Soon a feeling unlike any other will come over you: "This is me. This is what is best in me. I *want* to do this. I *have* to do this. Sacrifice? I might have thought so at first, but really, you have to be kidding. I am getting so much more from this than I ever could give."

How many of you who ever built a home for or served meals to the homeless, helped a child learn to read and study, or tried to bring peace to your community have had this feeling? Not that you necessarily did anything dramatic or earth-shaking, but something happened, something important to *you*, something that you wanted to continue to experience. Your Second to Last Chapter offers you the opportunity to make this not an occasional event but a continuing state of being that you may never have known before.

Could this not be called "selfish selflessness"? A play on words, I admit, but it happens to be true — doing good feels good, helping others feels right. Our actions are in line with what is best within us. The soft radiance of our soul's light, unobstructed, bathes us in an unimaginably warm glow. It is not quite peace or contentment, or even a sense of accomplishment. The best I can do is to use that term I fall back on: *allrightness*.

While we intuit that feeling so deeply and surely — whatever we might call it — the scientific world, never one to jump unthinkingly on any spiritual bandwagon, backs us up with hard data. They show that pleasure centers in our brain light up not only when we have sex or dig into a luscious chocolate torte (they certainly do), but when we help others (they certainly do as well).

Selfish selflessness. Once we experience what helping others does for *us*, we then want more of it. We realize there is no other direct path to this unique feeling (not even that chocolate torte), and we seek opportunities to produce it. We are *selfish*, we want to feel that warm glow again.

But at the same time, we are equally *selfless*, stepping away from our personal needs and gratifications to make someone else's life better. It is *not* only the warm fuzzies that we seek; we also truly want to make a difference, to help someone who needs help, to make the world a little better place before we, as Shakespeare said, "shuffle off this mortal coil."

What is it? It's a feeling of aliveness like nothing I've ever experienced in my professional career. Look, I've had my share of successes and triumphs. They all pale by comparison.

Judy Girard, President emeritus of the Food and HGTV Networks, who is creating a single-sex academy for girls in poverty in Wilmington, North Carolina

Your quest for happiness

At last count, Amazon.com had no fewer than 43,000 books that addressed the issue of happiness. Courses on happiness crop up in college course selections, learned studies delve into who is happy, why and how, and talk shows mine this rich vein of the human quest. If there is so much written, talked, and thought about happiness, why do so many people remain unsatisfied? Putting aside the true grumps, the ones who wouldn't be happy if joy were handed to them on a silver platter, this leaves millions of good, empathetic people who are…well, sort of happy, somewhat happy, mostly happy. But they are not really *fulfilled*. Something is missing. Perhaps you are one of them. I know I was, but I didn't know it until I found Homes of Hope.

Stop seeking happiness and let happiness find you.

You may still be confused about how you are going to be effective, about how you can possibly right the wrongs you have found, about how to start Your Second to Last Chapter. But as for being unsatisfied or unfulfilled, well, you won't have much time for those emotions once you do begin. You will have found a new purpose for your life and your day will be filled with flirting with great dreams and seeing great possibilities. You will constantly be "shopping," but you will be shopping for ways to make your dreams a reality. What a blessing it will be for you to have a reason to wake up each morning and go through the day alert and engaged, thinking about and seeking out the ideas, people, and resources you need to succeed.

Your Second to Last Chapter will be a time when meaning replaces ambition. You will have found *your* meaning. You will have given up *your* ambition and replaced it with a much bigger one,

one you will share with a large and growing number of what I call "SLCs."

It is not that SLCs don't have ambition; we surely do. But it is now focused outward, not inward. And once that shift is made, we soon discover that in fact our ambition has not lessened, it has increased. I don't exactly know how to explain this, but SLCs discover that there is a certain disembodied quality to what we do: we are intensely involved and yet we view our involvement from a distance. This is not the "us" we knew in our working life, where our ambition drove us to achieve for ourselves and our families. And when we did achieve, it was good for us in many ways. But now that achievement has another dimension to it. It is not achievement for its own sake, but for what good it can do, how it can benefit someone else, how it can make the world a little better place.

If this paradox of selfish selflessness is beginning to make some sort of sense, then you are almost there. What else can I say to help you make the jump?

You spread the selfish selflessness virus.
It's catching, so be careful.

Within each human being is a smorgasbord of emotional tendencies: jealousy, selfishness, pride, anger, empathy, kindness, generosity, courage. What shapes and triggers these tendencies is an equally wide range of factors, from family upbringing to culture and environment to the mechanics and physiology of neurotransmitters and our individual and shared DNA makeup.

And we all know that the actions of people we are with — and even beyond specific things they *do*, more who they *are* (call it their karma or aura) — influence us greatly. As Dacher Keltner, a professor of psychology at the University of California, Berkeley (and author of *Born to be Good: The Science of a Meaningful Life*) is quoted in *A Path Appears* by Nicolas D. Kristof and Sheryl WuDunn: "When people are around the Dalai Lama, people are like 'I feel different. I feel like giving stuff away.'"

The miracles of Second to Last Chapter work will amaze you. This "virus" spreads because what we SLCs are doing — a natural, human response to human need — immediately resonates with people. Like the stone thrown onto a still pond, ripples radiate out. Or perhaps a better analogy would be a mirror, another kind of mirror. As you look at the Dalai Lama or Mother Theresa or Albert Schweitzer, the man in a crimson robe or a woman bedecked with a blue head scarf or the doctor with the stethoscope around his neck slowly morphs into...yes...you! Perhaps it happens only for a moment, just for a flicker, but it happens. That is the impulse SLCs feel in the presence of people who have given themselves over to a higher calling. We want to participate in whatever it is that makes that man or woman so compelling. We sense that unspoken, quiet power. We do not want only to absorb its radiance, but we are moved to reflect it. I have seen this happen over and over again; let me just provide a few examples from Homes of Hope India.

+ A retired dentist volunteers to go to India, does what he can with the few instruments he had left from his practice. Little girls smile because they no longer feel tooth pain they lived with every day. On his return home, the dentist finds he wants to do more, but he realizes that any dentist going to India will be in the same situation as he was without more and better instruments. He tells his story to a fellow dentist, who is about to close his practice. Might he ask him for a few instruments, if he can spare them? "Take the whole office, I'm retiring," says his friend. Our dentist is stunned. Homes of Hope has just been given a three-chair dental office, with everything from x-ray machines to waste baskets.

* Homes of Hope had never thought of starting a dental clinic, but the need was certainly there. The problem is that the equipment is in Wilmington, North Carolina, and the ships that go to India sail out of Charleston, South Carolina. A beer distributor who hears of the project volunteers to truck the equipment to Charleston. Seven (donated) pallets are packed, taken in a Miller High Life-emblazoned truck to Charleston, put in a container, and sent by sea to India. The shipping costs somehow materialize.

* One of our board members is speaking at a parish in Kansas City and a woman comes up to him: "I'm a dentist; any use for me?" She's soon on a plane to India, meets the shipment, sets up the dental office, and takes care of its first patients.

Dr. Cathy Taylor-Osborne, our first dentist

⁺ A surfer hears of our work; his group takes physically challenged kids surfing. He looks at me; I look at him: orphan girls? India? Why not? Now, each year, surfers travel almost ten thousand miles from America to take dozens of orphan girls on a surfing safari. Little did it matter to those surfers that the girls couldn't swim and had never seen a large body of water. The surfers didn't know any good surfing beaches in India, where they would stay, or how they would raise the funds to get there. Minor details. Now, during the summer vacation that normally is the worst and loneliest time of the year — as other school children go home — Homes of Hope orphan girls experience the power of the ocean, actually "walk on water" and give their self-confidence a huge boost. The surfers come back year after year...actually because they can't stay away. A prime example of selfish selflessness.

Indo Jax® surfers from Wilmington, North Carolina, take girls on a surfing safari every year.

‣ A scientist goes to India for a conference, visits one of our schools, and funds a new science lab. Rotary Club members hear of our work and twenty-five solar-powered water purifiers later, a hundred thousand people have clean water to drink. Church members hear a talk about our work on the protein deficiency at one of our rural locations and a few months later, three cows are delivered. A grade school hears about the Home of Hope need for a playground and raises funds to build one.

For this emptiness is also a kind of fullness, and this stillness is not dead or inert. It is filled with infinite possibilities and stands poised in expectation of their fulfillment, with no comprehension of what that fulfillment may be and no desire for it to take any special preconceived form or direction.

Thomas Merton, *The Inner Experience*

Donated science equipment brings new excellence to our schools.

No one "sought" happiness for themselves in any of these ex-amples, but happiness came to that scientist and those dentists, surfers, students. That's what SLC work is all about: spreading the contagion of the pure enjoyment of making something wonderful happen to someone in need.

Although Donald Trump may not have had us in mind when he wrote *The Art of the Deal*, that is exactly what we practice. We SLCs are constantly looking for that "deal," something that will make someone's life better, safer, healthier, and yes, happier. We do not seek that "deal" for our own benefit, and yet what benefits we receive! Meaning has replaced ambition or, better put, our ambi-tion now has a new meaning.

Most of the things we humans think make us happy don't...altruists seemed disproportionately likely to age gracefully and maintain their health...a willingness to help others seemed more important to longevity than cholesterol levels...there was little connection between amounts spent on oneself and happiness...we mislead ourselves into thinking that we'll be happier spending on ourselves and acquiring material objects, while actually we may be wired to gain more pleasure from giving to others... survival of the kindest.

Nicholas Kristof and Sheryl WuDunn, *A Path Appears*

Here is what "pure" ambition looks like: It is the pure joy of a girl born with a harelip, who had lived in the shadows, never expecting to marry, proudly showing off her smiling two-year-old son.

Homes of Hope surgery for Susheela changed her life.

Something deep inside you will awaken if you pursue Your Second to Last Chapter, something you may or may not have experienced this exquisitely before. But wait, you always knew it was there, hidden perhaps, but there. It happens when your soul connects with the ground of all being, that great power of love that has waited patiently for this moment in your life so you might experience a feeling of oneness, completeness, unity like no other. Truly, *this* is *your* prime time.

WHY WE RESIST

Incline the ear of your heart.

Rule of Saint Benedict

Saint Benedict's wise and wonderful words encouraged his monks to listen for God's voice so they might grow spiritually. But we are not in the cloister in the sixth century, and God's voice is often not accessible to most of us in the twenty-first. And, once we are brave enough to "incline the ear of our heart" to the needs of the world, we often still hear a cacophony of voices. One of the major reasons we don't embark on new and meaningful work at our stage in life is that we are overwhelmed by the needs. Starving children in Africa, discarded widows in India, rampant disease in South America, millions of refugees in the Middle East…and right on our doorstep, children going to school hungry every day, soaring unemployment rates for marginalized young men, prisoners languishing in jails without hope…. I don't need to continue; just read the front page of today's newspaper.

I can remember so well my days in New York when I was in my mid-to-late thirties. I was free of any encumbrance, free to do anything I wanted. I could go to any place in the world as a reporter. I could tackle any social need as a crusading journalist.

What did I do with all this freedom? Nothing. I was paralyzed by the options; I exercised none of them. Only when I married Tracy (something I feared would severely limit my options and condemn me to a banal life, complete with requisite minivan and car seats) and began to lead a normal life did I write as I never wrote before. Then, more recently, I was fortunate to find my calling for My Second to Last Chapter on a pretty ordinary, touristy trip to India.

And now I am taking this perhaps audacious and certainly presumptuous step of trying to help you prepare for Your Second to Last Chapter. I do this for several reasons. First, if what I am saying doesn't resonate with you, you have probably stopped reading this book already. So, no harm there, except maybe the price you paid for the book (which you can give as a gift to someone else who you think wants to discover his or her own calling). Besides, Homes of Hope will benefit from the sales of this book, so thanks for the donation!

Second, I have been given a modest gift for writing, so why wouldn't I use it on such an important issue as this? The world needs more SLCs, so perhaps I can help a few more of you take the leap. I realize that many people discover meaningful work for the later years in life without any help from Paul Wilkes, but if I am talking to *you*, let's continue.

This is the main lesson I can offer as you approach Your Second to Last Chapter: Go about your regular life; be open, not anxious; and don't expect the voice to be heard this afternoon. In the very act of being open, you will be listening. And when you are quiet and listening to your inner self — isn't that when breakthrough insights are most likely to occur?

At our age, we are not listening so much for information as for transformation, for meaning, for legacy. We can endlessly debate the factual side of the world's needs, rattle off the statistics, cite the examples. We can *empathize* until the cows come home, but *transformation* is completely different. One sentence in a newspaper, one image in a television report…in my case, that one smile by a little girl…something, someone will strike a chord like nothing before. It will be a voice different from the rest. It will usually not be loud or demanding; it will be more of an invitation.

Let's get a little more specific and discuss some questions that might be on your mind right now.

At 50, I failed. I wanted to retire and "give back," but I didn't quite know how to do this. All I knew how to do was work. So I went back to work, ran some businesses, and made more money. It was fun, but not very satisfying. I finally got there at 58. I had to stop resisting and start to say "yes" to opportunities to serve that came my way. But this was the same me, and the talents I had in my business life translated into my new venture to rebuild a hospital in Africa.

Dale Smith, retired business executive

You fear "it" will take over your life.

Well, "it" might. But you might enjoy that.

Or, "it" will take over a part of your life, and you will enjoy that as well.

Either way, "it" will take time and work — that is if you expect "it" to flourish and really amount to something. Again, what we are talking about is not casual volunteer work, which is also a good thing and critically needed and what most people do at this stage in their lives. Organizations that do good things — from collecting for food pantries to reading for the blind to driving cancer patients to treatments — depend on an army of volunteers, each of whom allots a few hours that add up to meet the needs of the group. Don't ever say that Paul Wilkes put down such work. But it is not what I am talking about in this book. I am talking about something more ambitious, more of a commitment, more life-changing (both to you and to the people you seek to help). SLCs not only want to help, they want to change the world.

Women come up to me all the time: "I want to do something like you're doing, something that matters." But then as we talk, the trip to Barbados, the luncheons, the husband, the grandchildren, the fluff stuff and the real stuff, come tumbling in. They want it on their own schedule, at their convenience. Simple fact: It just doesn't work that way.

Judy Girard, President emeritus of the Food and HGTV Networks, who is creating a single-sex academy for girls in poverty in Wilmington, North Carolina

What I am talking about in Your Second to Last Chapter is a step, a big step. You might be starting an organization, or helping an existing organization branch out in a new direction, or replicating an organization that already exists and is a good model

for what you want to do in another place, or starting new initiatives under the umbrella of an existing organization (as I do with Homes of Hope with the Salesian sisters, who actually administer the orphanages and schools we support in India).

This is not volunteering; this a calling, a mission, a vocation. It is a job at which you want to work seriously for a good part of your remaining productive years, a challenge you are ready to take on without looking back. It is based on the discovery of something within you that will not be satisfied by anything less than your very best effort. You have found a need you want to address, a wrong you want to make right, something that both resonates in your core and insistently calls out to you. This is not a generic cause or need and, of course, there is no generic "you." You are being called to marshal the inner strength and maintain the staying power to, yes, we can use these words: Make a Difference in the World.

I can write those words only in retrospect. If you would have put those words before me as I stumbled through the early days of Homes of Hope, with no more grand a plan than to buy thirty mattresses so kids wouldn't have to sleep on a concrete floor, I would have thanked you for your kindness but told you to find somebody else to fit that bill, not me.

Homes of Hope gradually took over my life, but — full disclosure — I was a willing victim. I found working to build orphanages — supplying them with clean drinking water, computers, buses, jeeps, whatever was needed — to be enormously satisfying to me. But beyond that, it was great fun — "The Art of the Deal" — putting the needed pieces together to help those kids have a better life.

What could be a better thing to do with my life than that? Once you find the project that pierces your heart, you will have a new kind of power you never knew you had. How it happens I have never quite figured out, but it does.

Homes of Hope is now my "job," every day. I have never experienced this much enjoyment and can't wait to get to the computer each morning to see what has happened in India overnight, to see who has come forward to help. Also, I get to see where we are falling short and need to recalibrate our efforts.

My wife, Tracy, and I still take vacations, go to movies, spend time together, visit with our kids; in other words, we have a pretty normal life. It's just that my current and unpaid employment is Homes of Hope, and I know it will be until I can no longer be of help.

This image below about finding purpose in life might say it better than words, with just a little editing. In the part "You Are Paid for It," you can add something like "...in ways I never could have dreamed."

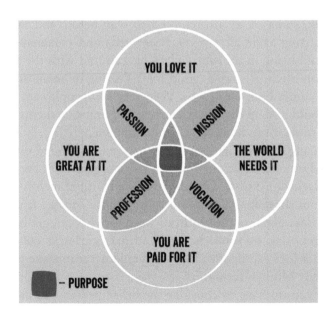

Now, I understand that you may not want to be completely taken over by your project, as I have been. That is perfectly understandable. But I also have to be honest by telling you that if you are going to make a real difference it is going to involve sacrifice and at times putting your own needs aside. You'll sort out how much you want to be "taken over" by it, but you definitely will be to some extent.

You don't know if your significant other wants to go along.

There are two ways of looking at this issue, and it can be a point of contention. The first is that this is your project and yours alone. The second is that this is your project and your partner can participate as much as he or she wants to.

Look, some of us are tempted to wax heroic and fantasize about casting aside all our material needs and personal attachments and living in the worst place we can find with the poorest people on earth. It sounds good for a fleeting moment and then real life comes back into focus. Very, very few people can, will, or even should give up their lives entirely and immerse themselves in a worthwhile work, however urgent and noble.

Actually that isn't necessary, as I have happily found out.

I did wax heroic at one point in my life, gave away everything I had, clothed myself in cast offs, and lived with homeless men. It was one of the unhappiest periods in my life. Today, I live a very middle class life, buy the clothes I need, drive a car, get haircuts, swim every day, walk on the beach, drink Starbucks coffee, and eat Trader Joe's excellent toffee. You would never mistake me for a martyr. Or Mother Teresa.

But you do have to consider the other person you are living

with — spouse, significant other, or good friend. You may have felt the call, but that does not mean she or he has to — or needs to.

In my case, although Tracy was with me when I first met Reena and Homes of Hope was born, this is not her way of using her talents. She goes with me to India, participates in functions, gives an occasional talk, but that's it. I can always call on her for advice, but I am very careful not to try to drag her into Homes of Hope work. The Homes of Hope office is in a back room of our home, and I try to respect the fact that we share a house but not Homes of Hope…at least to the degree that I am involved. That is the way it should be, at least for us.

If you are single, divorced, or widowed, a spouse will not be your problem, but others might: adult children, grandchildren, friends, even people in your church, synagogue, or mosque. For your family, the issue might be over money, but it might also be over concern for your well-being or just a genuine desire to have you around more. You will work through each of these situations.

No one really understands,
and you have no one to talk to about this.

Among even your closest family members or friends, you may find you don't have anyone to talk with about what is happening inside you. It may be an uncomfortable or seemingly too idealistic a subject (i.e., making a difference in the world) and you may be reluctant or shy about sharing your thoughts. You may be known as a hard-charging executive or someone who has worked quietly at a job for years, never once mentioning those "murmurs of the soul" we've been discussing.

Don't worry, you're not alone. This is not a usual conversation at most cocktail parties, on the eighth tee, or during family gatherings.

When I really got involved with rebuilding the hospital in Sierra Leone, and especially when cancer came into my life, some of my friends said I was nuts. But they don't get it, this is what gets my blood circulating. If you've been a problem solver all your life, why stop? They've got their boats and golf, but that just didn't fit for me.

Dale Smith, retired business executive

Within your professional, social, or religious circles, if you think about it, you will probably come upon someone who could be the right person to talk with. It may not be someone you know well, however, or with whom you have shared any sort of personal knowledge. Instinctively you will sense that this is someone who has an ability to listen and help you make sense of what is going on inside you.

In case you are wondering how such a person might react to your request, "to talk things over about a direction in life I'm thinking about" (you'll say it much better than that), they will be complimented that you thought enough of them to ask. I know because I had two or three react to me in that way.

We go to all sorts of specialists for everything from a cranky shoulder to not enough memory on our computer, why not find a listening and discerning person who can help in this case? It could be a professional therapist or counselor, but it need not be. A compassionate, intelligent advisor — especially for something as profound as your quest for a meaningful pursuit in this part of your life — may come from a strange place in your life. But once you sit down and start talking, it will become clear that she or he is the right person. It is sort of unquantifiable, but there will be an inner authority in that person that will echo in your own heart.

You really wonder if you have
this much "juice" left in you.

I have been working since I was ten years old, when I got my first newspaper route. I had to work in factory jobs and drive a truck to make my way through college. After the Navy, I wrote for a couple of newspapers, then began my freelance writing life. I taught writing part time. There was never a time in my life that I didn't work. Some of the jobs were exciting, some were for survival. With some, the "juice" was flowing; other times not so much.

I do get more tired now than I did at 30 or 40; my short nap after lunch is a mandate. My concentration is probably not as keen; fog clouds my brain a bit more than in my younger life. But, trust me, the "juice" is still there and wants to flow.

When you are doing something that might not be done unless *you* do it, when you are in alignment with what is best within you, there is an energy you didn't even know was there. Why? Because your mind and your soul don't have to work through layers of meaning to address something that truly matters. This does. For those of you who have children, even if they are now adults, think about the energy you have when your kids suddenly are in trouble or really need you. Wasn't the "juice" flowing, no matter how tired you might have been a few minutes earlier?

Some recent studies have shown that, while our processing speed is slower (it actually peaks in our late teens) and our ability to remember names (that peaks in our early twenties) or manipulate numbers (early thirties) is sometimes sketchy, our ability to navigate tricky situations and read people's moods remains in wonderful shape late in life. Brain cells may be dying and mental operations slowing, but as Elkhonon Goldberg writes in *The Wisdom Paradox*, "What I have lost with age…I seemed to have gained in my capacity of instantaneous, almost unfairly easy, insight." In other words, while it is true that certain of our powers are dulled with age, others actually sharpen.

Let's be honest. At this point in our lives, unlike any other time, we often don't have to do anything some days. For some women and men, who have lived active, involved lives, this is a terrifying void. And some will fill it with meaningless activities, or drinking too much, or some kind of forced pursuit or pastime or hobby, just to get through the day.

Again, this is not to say you shouldn't play golf, raise bonsai trees, or play with your grandchildren. All are very good things. But if there is something else nudging at your edges, flickering onto your semi-conscious stage as you fall asleep or awaken, something that comes to you as you pray or meditate or walk in the woods… that is a sign that there is still something out there for you to do.

And once you begin to do that thing, power rises up from within. Your soul knows no bounds, no limits. It seeks your true freedom and in that freedom is a capacity, a potential, to live with a fullness you may never have experienced before.

You don't have a clear idea of how to proceed.

One of my spiritual mentors, the nineteenth-century Cardinal John Henry Newman, said, "A real idea is equivalent to the sum total of its possible aspects." Now that statement can be confusing and intimidating, until we look at it closely. What the good cardinal is saying is that there will be many ways to make what will usually be a small and dim glimmering of an idea into real and useful work. Every aspect will not be explored, every option will not be exercised. Only the one that speaks to you. It will find you.

And those aspects of the idea will unfold slowly, but to the predisposed mind they will begin to take shape and develop. Our ideas, given freedom, are living things...they speak to us.

As you will read in the next chapter, Homes of Hope developed slowly over a period of time, time during which many, many needs continually arose, each of them compelling and urgent. I found I had to see what I could do to meet some of those and to see that others were beyond my reach. I did not explore every aspect of the idea. I just did the most urgent things I could do. Which, in turn, turned out to be the most possible for me to achieve.

Once I was walking on the monastery grounds at Mepkin Abbey in South Carolina, where I periodically visit to refocus my life and reconnect with God. It was early morning and dark and I worried that I would stray off the path. But here was one small wayside light that, when reached, brought into dim view another light, and when that light was reached, the next came into view. I couldn't see all of them, just one light at a time. I always remember that lesson in my Homes of Hope work: one step at a time. I may not see too far down the road, but I can always see enough for the next step.

But we cannot live the afternoon of life according to the program of life's morning — for what was great in the morning will be little at evening, and what in the morning was true will at evening become a lie.

C. G. Jung, *Modern Man in Search of a Soul*

ONE EXAMPLE:
MY SECOND TO LAST CHAPTER

*I offer the story of Homes of Hope as an example of what Second to Last Chapter work can look like. **It is only one example.** You may find your calling in your community, within another organization, or with a program that you can replicate. There are many other paths, many approaches. This is mine. You can skip this chapter if you want. It is not the purpose of the book; it is offered only as a concrete example of the kind of thing **you** could do.*

When I returned to the United States in early 2006, I was haunted by the grinding poverty I had witnessed in India…and by Reena. I began to tell my friends about meeting Reena, her story, my reaction…and the smile I couldn't forget. I found myself relating the story over and over, almost compulsively, to anyone who would listen. At first, I thought I was overstepping my bounds, wearing my heart on my sleeve, but I could see that Reena's story made the same impact on others it had made on me. A helpless child, lost, kidnapped, then brutally blinded to make her a "better beggar." Destitute conditions, seventy-five girls, each with her own appalling background of poverty, abuse, neglect. I could see the look on people's faces — they were stunned by the cruelty. They were ready to help, to do something, but I didn't know what to ask for, what to tell them to do. After all, I wasn't a charity. I had no "there" there. I was merely a man retelling a horrific story.

My mind kept going back to that concrete floor where Reena and the other children slept each night on a thin straw mat. I saw a possibility. That Christmas, I sent out a letter to my friends, asking them to contribute $100 for "A Bed for Reena." We would buy mattresses and coverlets so the girls could at least get off that hard concrete floor. I collected about $3,000. It was a start. And, as it would turn out, a foolish one.

I eagerly traveled back to India early the next year with the money. I drove into the city of Kochi with Sister Sophy and found that with $3,000 I could buy seventy-five foam mattresses and material for coverlets. The mattresses would have to be custom cut to a smaller size than the standard, both because they would be used for children and would take up less space where they slept.

It took a few days for the mattresses to be made, and in those few days staying at the orphanage I began to look more deeply into the lives of Reena and her friends. I sat with them at dinner time and watched as they ate a huge mound of white rice topped with just a hint of a vegetable curry. I looked at their skinny arms and legs, collar bones protruding, sores on their skin. These girls were terribly malnourished. I guessed at their ages and was always three or four years off—always thinking they were younger than they were. Because of their lack of nutrition from the moment of their conception, they all were stunted for their age.

One of the mothers, a trash picker, came by to see her three daughters, Alice, Anju, and Ancy, who were in the care of the sisters. She and the three girls had been living on the streets since her drunken husband abandoned the family, a common occurrence I found out, especially when daughters were concerned. Girls were not even considered second class; they were no class at all. A common wish for young brides was, "May you be the mother of a hundred sons," underscoring the preference for male offspring. Men walked away from wives who bore them only daughters, considering them cursed, and women who were already poor and struggling became destitute and homeless. Three growing and beautiful young girls were tempting targets as the mother plied the streets in search of trash. Sexual abuse, rape, and the kidnapping of young girls to sell into prostitution rings were all too common occurrences in the slums of Kochi. The sisters finally convinced the reluctant mother that her girls would be safe and well-cared for at Home of Hope.

Their mother had parked her rickety cart by the gate. She was a tiny, painfully thin woman, weighing no more than eighty pounds and wearing a thread-bare but colorful sari. Her hair was neatly combed. I could see she was putting on the best face she could for her children. The cart was heaped with plastic bottles, cardboard, and rags she had scavenged from people's garbage. It reeked of decayed food and crawled with insects. This was the life these girls faced if they were not in the care of the sisters. To survive, they too had once been rag pickers and would grow up to be rag pickers if not for the sisters and Home of Hope.

The Salesian sisters were doing a heroic job, but the classrooms in the adjoining school were bare and crowded, with 50 or 60 children jammed in, some taking turns sitting on the floor because there were not enough seats. The few computers were ancient; half were broken. I started drawing up a list of needs. I stopped. They needed everything from daily food to even the basics of school supplies. I refocused on the mattresses; at least *that* I could do. Or so I assumed.

I was so proud when the mattresses were delivered, the coverlets sewn, and the girls admired their new beds. For many of them it was the first time in their life they had not slept on the hard ground.

My ill-fated mattresses still earned a big smile from Reena.

The next day, my happy little bubble burst. If there was barely enough room to store their thin straw mats during the day, these much larger mattresses posed an even greater problem. The space allotted to them along the wall in the sleeping area was already crowded and the floor too dirty to keep the coverlets clean. One night and a pile of dirty bed sheets later, the sisters, girls, and I smiled at each other and knew it wasn't going to work this way. We would have to wait until the girls had bunk beds to sleep in, a building that housed their dormitory.... Wait, I'm getting ahead of the story here. I hadn't yet formally started Homes of Hope. I hadn't yet promised that I would find the money to build them a new orphanage building. But I was about to.

My Second to Last Chapter work was beginning to take shape. I was depressed at what I was seeing, yet energized by the heartfelt response I had gotten from my friends in the United States. The sisters and girls were thankful for my well-intentioned but ill-planned first project. They had seen so many visitors come... and so many visitors go. They could not put too much hope in me. I had that hope, however, and I pressed on.

When I returned to the United States, I sat in my quite nice office in the library of the University of North Carolina at Wilmington looking out over the campus, the well-trimmed hedges, and the newly mown grass bisected by crisp walkways. Just like my life: neat and orderly. I wanted to do so much for the girls in India, but with my teaching schedule I knew I would be severely limited. Time, there just wasn't enough time. That night I looked at my bank statement for the last pay period. I found the form the Social Security Administration had sent me earlier in the year, informing me what I would receive if I started collecting retirement benefits now — I had just turned sixty-seven and a half.

It would not be as much in dollars, but in hours? Time — unlimited, uninhibited time — would be mine. My needs were simple. My kids were gone. My wife would understand — I hoped. I turned in my resignation, effective at the end of the semester. And in a few months, for the first time in my mature life, I had no job… paying job that is. I had had fancy titles: distinguished visiting professor, author, journalist. Now I was just Paul.

Vocation is where our greatest passion meets the world's greatest need.
Frederick Buechner

Suddenly I had no standing, no title, no credentials. I was just a man with a story and a dream, a pretty fuzzy dream at the time, to help Reena and her friends to a future better than their horrible past. I filled out the papers to form a 501c3 nonprofit organization, leaving the top blank. Well, whatever it was, it needed a name.

Prathyasha Bhavan — emblazoned on a sign atop the wall on Binny Road — was the Malayalam name of the orphanage where I found Reena in Kochi. That translates into Home of Hope. It seemed a perfect, positive, and forward-looking name for an organization dedicated to the welfare of orphaned, neglected, and abandoned girls.

I called India. I must have been in daze, or possessed. What gave me the audacity to say what I did? "Sister, get an architect and start planning the orphanage. I'm going to help you." I couldn't believe what I had just said. But there it was. There was no turning back now.

My first effort, the bed for Reena, was presented on no more than a single sheet of paper and an email message I sent to a group of friends. I quickly realized I had to both tell the story better and legitimize what I was doing. Home of Hope needed a website.

Today, you can go to our website www.homeofhopeindia.org and see our approach, which I employed right from the beginning. We accentuate the positive. While I ache over the pictures of emaciated children that we often see in a lot of fund-raising material, I don't like feeling I am being guilt-tripped and dragged into making a contribution or a commitment of time. And I don't think other people like it either. Yes, our website and the brochure I created include photos and stories of the life our girls experienced before they came into our care, but I didn't want that to be the emphasis.

I needed to put a "face" on Home of Hope. In fact, faces. I wanted potential donors and volunteers to see and know our girls. When I began to collect more of the girls' stories, I found myself both enraged by what they had suffered and all the more determined to help them.

Mahalakshmi's mother was a prostitute, and so Mahalakshmi herself was offered as a child prostitute at the age of eight. Maria was abandoned under a bridge at the age of four. Rajeswari was begging with her mother in a train station and they started running away from the police. Her mother was killed by on oncoming train, after which her father committed suicide. Asha was dumped into a trash bin by her drunken father. I matched those stories to the faces of the girls I was beginning to know at Home of Hope.

How could these precious girls be smiling today after what they had been through? We in the United States simply had to help them get proper food, a proper home, schooling. And I wanted our donors to know what their support would mean in their lives. I wanted them look into the faces of the girls and know what they had been through...and what might be their future with our help.

I am hardly a shy person; in my forty years as a journalist I have asked people for the most intimate details of their lives...but to ask for money? I grimaced. But then something strange happened when I got up to talk before a group of people. I found it was no different than telling the story of Reena to a friend. After all, this wasn't actually *me* asking for money. *He* — that guy who went to India and looked into the face of a tiny, blinded girl who changed his life — *he* was doing the asking. But *he* happened to be *me!*

I spoke in churches, to Rotary and Civitan clubs, women's groups, pottery co-ops, book clubs.... I went wherever I was invited, or could invite myself. With each talk, the circle widened, the word about Home of Hope began to circulate in Wilmington, North Carolina, where Tracy and I live.

I tried to think of ways people could be more linked to the girls, beyond writing a check. When a person sponsored one of our girls for a year ($300), they received a mug with that girl's image and background information about her life. The same for a year's sponsorship ($1,000) of one of our girls going on to higher education. Periodically, I would tell the donors of the girl's progress...or her difficulties. Our sponsors would grow up with their girl. Yes, we have a mission statement, but I believe it is the human stories, the faces, that really count.

Our 501c3 status was granted by the IRS and, as I watched the bank account grow, I couldn't quite believe what was happening. People were responding...responding tremendously. I began wiring money to India; donations reached $50,000. There's nothing better to test your faith — and to draw in donors — than to make a commitment to build a building, start it, and then not have the money to finish it.

It took another year, but the new Home of Hope was nearing complete funding, almost $200,000. My work in India would soon be over, my pledge fulfilled: Reena would soon have a real home and sleep in a real bed. As I prepared to go to India for the dedication of the building, I received an international phone call. It was from Stuart Padley, a Microsoft executive who had heard my talk at his Seattle parish and had agreed to be on our small board of directors. He was on a business trip to the Microsoft office in Hyderabad and somehow found that another group of Salesian sisters, from the same order that worked in Kochi, maintained a home for girls in Secunderabad, Hyderabad's twin city.

There was static on the line and he had to repeat himself a few times. "Horrible conditions" "Concrete floor...sleeping" "Bad, Paul, really bad; worse than Kochi, far worse." "We've got to do something."

I would later find that Stuart was standing on the second floor of a rented building in Secunderabad, surrounded by almost a hundred street children, more than I had found at Kochi. They, too, were sleeping on the floor, but it was so crowded that four or five had to huddle together and share a single blanket.

Out on the mean streets of Hyderabad and Secunderabad, traffickers trolled for young girls, kidnapping them and sending them off to a life of horrid degradation as prostitutes or domestic slaves. Some of the girls were living on a garbage heap, scavenging for food, when the sisters found them. There were tiny children who didn't know their age; some didn't even know their name.

They had been brought up entirely on the streets, living in train stations and bus stands.

I would gradually find out that the orphanage in which I had found Reena was only one of three that the Salesian Sisters administered in the three South Indian states of Kerala, Karnataka, and Andra Pradesh. The sisters had divided India into six provinces; this was called the Bangalore Province. The sisters also ran hostels and schools, educating some 20,000 children, most of them poor. Additionally, they worked with impoverished villagers, with a special emphasis on single mothers whose husbands had abandoned them or had died. In every location, the water was undrinkable. The schools were badly in need of basic supplies, books, computers. All of the Salesian sisters' sites were struggling just to meet day-to-day needs. Medicines for sick children were in short supply, and most of the children were badly malnourished. The list went on.

I stared at my phone after the call from Stuart was cut off. I was standing in the vestibule at a Catholic parish between masses. In an hour, I would be thanking people for helping us complete the promised orphanage at Kochi. And then I realized that my work wasn't over in India. It had just begun.

It didn't take much soul-searching, to be honest. Something wonderful was happening. Home of Hope — because of my work as a somewhat unstructured but spontaneous and impassioned organizer (when thanked, I called myself the "hollow pipe" through which donations flowed, nothing more) and the work and generosity of hundreds of people — had a life of its own. It simply wanted to grow. There was so much more that needed to be done, and I could see that the donors and people like Stuart who got involved with Home of Hope in those early days were experiencing something deep and important helping these resilient street girls and resourceful nuns. This work was not, as they say "heavy lifting," not at all. Most importantly, the sisters were extremely cooperative, didn't believe in bureaucracy, and were open to new ideas.

So, what was the issue? We were going forward.

Stuart Padley playing cards
with girls from the orphanage at Secunderabad

The dedication at Kochi in December of 2008 was a wonderful, festive event with a huge red horseshoe-shaped arch over the gate, banners streaming, officials giving long speeches in Malayalam, and girls grasping Tracy's and my hands to take us to see their gleaming white tile kitchen, study rooms with real desks, and best of all their beds. I watched as Bindu "practiced" lying in bed; she had never been in one before and needed to know how to get in and lie there. The girls were so happy, so proud. Especially Reena.

She sensed she had played a key role in my coming back and helping to build this gorgeous, three-story building. And she was right!

Doorway at Kochi orphanage, with names of benefactors

Home of Hope was now entering its third year and, as I had pledged to the sisters that we would build our second orphanage at Secunderabad, I added the "s" to our name. We were now Homes of Hope, and our goal for that second orphanage was set at an astounding $300,000. (Kochi had cost a third less because Paul Raj, the local construction manager, was a friend of the sisters.) As for my life...well, it had changed dramatically and it hadn't changed that much. I now had a wonderful, full time job at absolutely no pay. I was having the time of my life. I was loving it.

Along with that exhilaration, however, came something else. With each day, the picture in India became clearer. And more depressing. The sheer scope of the needs was like staring into a chasm, a chasm that would swallow me if I had the temerity to lean forward to peer into its murky depths.

The eighteen schools run by the sisters were barely hanging on, with more and more children unable to pay even the modest fees. They needed computers, language labs, audiovisual equipment, Internet access, drinkable water. I had to bring in more people, donors to meet material needs, volunteers to ease the burden in overcrowded classrooms and to teach English and computer skills — two keys critical to the students' future. I had no master plan, but I tried to steer whatever chance meetings and even vague possibilities I found into opportunities for our work in India.

Being open about what we were doing and hoping to do, and being honest in saying we often didn't know what direction we should take, conspired to not only widen the group of Homes of Hope supporters but also to take us places we never could have imagined.

♦ Early on, I was commenting to my younger son, Daniel, that if Homes of Hope was to thrive, I couldn't keep asking the same people for help. How to raise money without asking people for it? We were standing in front of a book case. Daniel had just completed a semester of college and told me about books he sold and bought on Amazon.com. What if we had people donate books they no longer needed to us and we sold them? The idea jelled. Jennifer Allen and Betty Harrison, a couple of book-loving volunteers, appeared (one, because of a talk I gave about meaningful work after retirement). We all pitched in the hundreds of books we knew we never would read again, asked friends for theirs, created an account on Amazon and became Used Books, New Lives. Fast forward: we make about $10,000 a year selling used books that people are happy to give us, and the books we can't sell we ship to India, approaching 450,000 at this writing. We have created or enriched libraries at all our eighteen schools, three orphanages, and eight hostels.

Our books are big hit in India.

+ I was talking to a surfer friend about the orphan girls in India and how their school vacation months of April and May were the loneliest. He did free surf camps for handicapped, autistic, even blind kids here in Wilmington. We looked at each other: India? Fast forward: Surfing Safari is a yearly event in India now, and besides surfing the girls go on elephant rides and stay in a comfortable beachside resort. They have been able to reclaim some of the childhood so cruelly deprived them. They can now just be kids on vacation.

+ I was at a benefit sponsored by the Wilmington Yoga Center for a group of Rwandan refugees. I made a donation, but I also passed along one of our brochures. Fast forward: each year Yoga enthusiasts go to Kochi to spend time with the girls and practice yoga, which, after all, originated in India.

+ We applied to foundations, including the Gates Foundation, but were routinely rejected. But that indefatigable Brit, Stuart Padley, talked up our work to his fellow employees, who have generously supported us (with Microsoft matching funds) and then helped to introduce our sisters in Bangalore to Microsoft engineers there, who have helped with computer education and maintenance. What a sight that was, to see seven brilliant computer guys and a Catholic nun, in full religious garb, sitting around a table in Microsoft's High Tech City's soaring glass office building.

+ I got an email from a woman whose husband worked in America for Infosys, the Indian global technology giant. Infosys periodically donated their used computers to non-profits who were working in poor schools. That was us, for sure. I supplied all the needed information and pretty much forgot about it. Not all promising or promised leads work out. A year later, ten perfectly good used computers showed up at our Bangalore school.

Corporate commuters get a new lease on life
at Homes of Hopes schools

◆ We were led to the First Hand Foundation, which funds
medical help and surgery for poor children. Fast forward:
On a recent visit to Bangalore, proud parents brought me
Deepika, their once-crippled daughter, to show how well
she is walking due to the physiotherapy paid for by First
Hand. We have been able to get grants for a girl with severe
diabetes, a boy who needed surgery to correct a life-threat-
ening kidney malfunction, and to dozens of other medically
needy children.

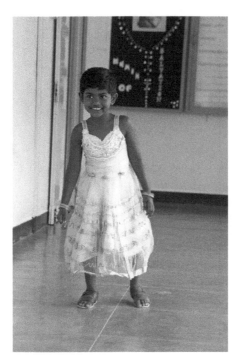

Deepika walking

I showed my slides to anyone who would look at them and, besides donating, people wanted to experience what I had and go to India and work in the orphanage. So we sent our first volunteers, eventually branding them *HopeCorps Volunteers*. Young college students and retired teachers, a house painter and a mural painter, a mother and her daughter, a mother and her son would eventually go to India for us. Our youngest volunteer was eight, the oldest eighty-five. They lived in our orphanages and schools, bringing their skills and enthusiasm to India and coming back changed forever.

My son Daniel is among the over 300 Homes of Hope volunteers who have gone to India.

Believe me, there were plenty of failures as well. I thought of training the girls to refurbish computers, but we couldn't get any computers to work on. Water purifiers did a great job of purifying, but the water was still so salty it was undrinkable. Shipments got held up in the bureaucratic tsunami that is Indian customs. My first volunteer came down with a horrible autoimmune disease. But, it always seemed that every project that failed was followed by three or four incredible and totally out-of-the-blue successes.

+ School kids in Ann Arbor, Michigan, raised funds to transform a dusty patch of land into a playground of swings and climbing bars.

• The sisters at our Bangalore orphanage badly wanted to create a marching band to build self-esteem and pride, but without uniforms and instruments that was pretty tough to bring off. PPD, an international pharmaceutical company with an office in Bangalore, not only donated funds to create the band, but their employees are now visitors and mentors for our girls.

• On a visit to one our rural locations near Mysore, I found ninety girls anemic, pitifully undernourished, their arms and legs like sticks. Three fine Holstein cows to the rescue, courtesy of a Seattle parish.

• No jeep; we'll get you a jeep. School bus needed to bring kids in from rural areas…ditto. Language lab, diesel generator? Great idea; how much? What do you mean, there's no money to send Pinky on to nursing school? Let's find somebody to sponsor her.

Cows produce little cows...and milk...
all because of a generous Seattle parish.

No more blackouts; our generator stands by,
ready to hum into action.

Our language lab in Kochi teaches English,
a critical skill for our girls' futures.

A Miracle Unfolding

That's what I have begun to call Homes of Hope, and that's exactly what it is: A Miracle Unfolding. I can't quite understand how this has all happened. I cannot believe it even as I type these words. But, this book is not just about my work. It is about *your* work as well. Your unique talents will produce your own miracles. You, too, will become a SLC (Second to Last Chapter) person.

As you look at the possibilities of Your Second to Last Chapter, two synergistic elements will be seeking each other. When *your passionate belief* to make the world a better place meets the *basic goodness and generosity of people,* that is the recipe with which miracles are made. People want to be part of something bigger than themselves, they are just waiting for the opportunity and the invitation. And, yes, there are hundreds of thousands of charities and good causes to work on, but only you might work on yours.

If you check back with me in a year from the writing of this book, I can almost guarantee that Homes of Hope will be under sail on other uncharted waters. And I'll probably have to report that something I'm planning right now, sure it will go smoothly, will have turned out to be a dismal failure.

But I also know that I will be telling you of unforeseen miracles that have unfolded.

SOME FINAL THOUGHTS

Let the words of Thomas Merton, whose spirit eventually drew me to India, say it better than I ever could:

Do not depend on the hope of results. You may have to face the fact that your work will be apparently worthless and even achieve no result at all, if not perhaps results opposite to what you expect. As you get used to this idea, you start more and more to concentrate not on the result, but on the value, the rightness, the truth of the work itself.

Thought One:
You have to be "indifferent" or "disinterested"
if you are going to succeed.

In his wisdom, Ignatius of Loyola, the founder of the Jesuits, offered a strange word of advice to those who would follow him in the revolutionary work his followers would do, not only preaching a religious faith but also shaping education in the sixteenth century. The word: *indifference*.

Rather than advocating a lackadaisical attitude, a "whatever" way of life (to put it in a more contemporary context), Ignatius viewed indifference as a key factor in both mental and spiritual health. To him indifference was a poised freedom that allowed his followers to constantly assess the situation around them, meanwhile giving them the time and liberty to discern the best tack to take. He would not allow his followers to sail along on a blissful dream of "being called" or "doing good" and therefore conclude that whatever they did or thought was exactly what Divine Providence had intended for them. Ignatius believed in emotion, so much so that he asked his followers to review their lives each night and to find what the consolations and desolations of that day were saying to them. But he would not let emotions run wild. Emotions would be an important factor, but not the only one, as their life circumstances presented often blurry options.

We can surmise that the Jesuits who sailed from Italy to India and China and South America could never be called "indifferent." They were passionate about what they were doing. But as they landed on foreign shores, whatever training or orientation they had received, spiritual depth they possessed, or personal abilities they exhibited all got tossed into the air. They had to choose what made sense at the time.

You, too, will be required to act with indifference or disinterest in Your Second to Last Chapter. The stakes will be different as there will be no profit or prestige motive, no career path to be followed. As you become a different kind of entrepreneur — an entrepreneur for good — you will experience a new kind of flexibility and liberation from the benchmarks of your previous years, a new freedom to dream and innovate as you search for ways to realize your own destiny.

> To be truly alive is to feel one's ultimate existence with one's daily existence.
>
> Christian Wiman, *My Bright Abyss*

Thought Two:
The quality of your effort,
not the sum total of your results,
is what really counts.

I am a results-driven individual. When I think hard, plan hard, and work equally hard, I expect to achieve my goal. Homes of Hope has taught me differently. I learned that two plus two may not equal four. It took at least the first three years of Homes of Hope before I was able not to crash and burn with every effort that failed. India is a very frustrating place to work. The bureaucracy is not only a miasma of red tape but seemingly heartless, even when trying to save the lives of these orphaned, abandoned, and neglected girls. Gradually I did begin to concentrate on the rightness, the truth of the work itself, and found myself pleasantly surprised when things worked out and not as devastated or angry when they didn't.

I believe that a principle like this — concentrating on the rightness rather than the result of our actions — that you will practice in Your Second to Last Chapter will have a broad impact on your life. You will become more patient (not always, trust me) and you will learn to allow the stars to align as they will rather than constantly trying to arrange them. You will find yourself concentrating as much on "how" you are doing something as "what" you are doing. You will almost be able to watch yourself — as if you were being filmed — and that is how you will know whether or not you are acting in a decent, humane manner. Just to ramrod something through to get the job done is guaranteed to leave you with an uneasy residue of shame.

Because after all, when you draw back and say: "I really tried my best, took stock of the options and circumstances, and gave it my best shot"…well, what more can you ask of yourself? Although most of us have thrived on winning, it is our losses that usually prove our measure.

Thought Three:
Discovering who you are, after all,
is your most important job.

I wind experiences around myself and cover myself with pleasures and glory like bandages in order to make myself perceptible to myself and to the world, as if I were an invisible body that could only become visible when something visible covered its surface.

Thomas Merton, *New Seeds of Contemplation*

I don't think Merton's idea is all that foreign to most of us; we have all struggled to "be somebody" only to experience a certain hollowness as we pursued goals that didn't line up with what was the best inside us. Your Second to Last Chapter affords you a chance for a new start, a new way of being. After all, who is trying to impress anyone anyhow at this point in life? Your ego, stripped bare, is a pure fountain of goodness. After all, that is your soul.

I believe that doing good makes us good. At a minimum, it makes us better. At a maximum, it makes us holy. I believe that listening and responding to the soft murmurs of our soul brings out something in us that perhaps lies dormant or at least is not fully realized. At this time of our lives, with nothing to prove to any-one (as if *they* would care!), with abundant time and a wonderful assemblage of talents, here is the chance to put aside the various masks we all wear and get down to being who we are.

I don't know what your destiny will be, but one thing I know: the only ones among you who will be really happy are those who will have sought and found how to serve.

Albert Schweitzer

Of course, taking on meaningful work is not going to forge a total makeover of our personality. If you lived in my house, you would see first-hand what an imperfect, impatient, erratic, irratio-nal, unloving clod of humanity that I too often can be. But the work that I do with Homes of Hope *disposes* me to be a better person. After all, I can't be trying to help orphan girls ten thousand miles away while being that clod, full time, in my daily life.

And another bonus on the mask removal front is that it pro-vides the freedom to talk about things that matter, about needs crying to be addressed, about wounds that should be bound up and healed. You will be surprised how daily interchanges begin to change when family and friends know what you are about. People want to talk about real life issues and you provide them with a perfect reason to do so. Stand by, cocktail party chit-chat, you're in for an overhaul.

> When any original act of charity or of gratitude…is presented either to our sight or imagination, we are deeply impressed with its beauty and feel a strong desire in ourselves of doing charitable and grateful acts also.
>
> Thomas Jefferson

Thought Four:
Your Second to Last Chapter
is a new way of walking in the world.

Once you begin to address human need, you are never the same again. As you take on Your Second to Last Chapter, a new sense of compassion, of understanding, will gradually seep in and around the edges of your preconceived ideas and disrupt your firmest prejudices. A rising level of compassion will find room in your heart for both those close to you and the stranger as well. And that compassion will also include you, a swirling, ever-changing accumulation of life experiences, sufferings, and achievements. You will take that person more seriously, listening to the voice within as it guides you.

You will know deep in your heart that you have responded to a human need that has called out to you, asking you to marshal and employ your skills, right now. You will feel a new sense of balance, not a free-floating sense of "am I doing enough?" You will know that you are.

There emerges a new understanding of the world, a powerful spiritual enthusiasm that shakes the very foundations of man's existence.

Rabbi Joseph Soloveitchik, *Halakhic Man*

As you embark upon Your Second to Last Chapter, you will find a new attitude for the rest of your life. You will find that problems are merely solutions not yet found; that the answer "no" certainly means "maybe" and is merely a way station en route to "yes." You will find a sense of abandon — not reckless at all — pervading your life. You will feel it with your family, your friends. Suddenly you will realize that you don't worry about the little things as much, partially because you have less time to do so, but mostly because you'll have major things to do.

Final Thought:
Your Path Ahead

And now I will stop trying to take over your life. Because that's exactly what I've been trying to do. I didn't say it in the introduction, because you might have stopped right there. But now that you have seen the possibilities Your Second to Last Chapter might hold, I hope that you will join with me and thousands of other SLCs and set about making this world a better place, in your own way...and on your own terms.

As you seek the work that will enflame your heart and call upon the talent, experience, and wisdom you have assembled thus far in your life — a friendly word: Don't be anxious. Be open, be eager, be ready. But do not be anxious. Because as you seek Your Second to Last Chapter, "it" is seeking you as well. Trust me; you will find each other. Vocation is the intersection of opportunity (need) and ability (talent). You will find your "it" if you look there.

There are three typical options you should consider, and I am sure there are many more variations.

1. **Start something entirely new.** Find something that does not exist right now but is exactly what the world needs and you can do. This is perhaps the hardest of the options, because you have to create something out of nothing. But it can be done and sometimes there is no other choice.

2. **Take something already existing and replicate it in your community.** My friend Judy Girard found young girls in poverty in our hometown of Wilmington, North Carolina, who needed mentors and a first class education if they were to thrive. Judy found that the Young Women's Leadership

Network had successfully created five schools for girls in poverty in New York City. She is bringing their program and approach to Wilmington.

3. **Work under an existing organization to address its needs.** This is what I have done with Homes of Hope. I found a group of Catholic nuns in India that were struggling to take care of and build new homes for orphaned, abandoned and neglected girls, and I am helping them do so.

Our website is **www.secondtolastchapter.com.** And you can email me at **paul@secondtolastchapter.com.** I hope you'll be in touch to ask questions or to share Your Second to Last Chapter story. If you do get in touch, I'll send you some steps you might want to consider as you approach Your Second to Last Chapter work. Thanks for reading this book, and blessings on whatever it is you choose to do with the rest of your life.

Let me end with words from Thomas Merton that continue to inspire me.

> *If you want to identify me,*
> *ask me not where I live*
> *or what I like to eat,*
> *or how I comb my hair*
> *but ask me what I think*
> *is keeping me from living fully*
> *for the thing I want to live for.*

APPENDIX

Resources

Here are just a few articles and websites to get you started and thinking about Your Second to Last Chapter.

As new material comes out frequently, you might want to do a web search. Put in some combination of "retirement," "meaning," and "purpose" (and similar words) and see what you come up with. And please share it on www.secondtolastchapter.com.

Articles

www.forbes.com/sites/mikelewis/2013/10/22/life-after-retirement/

www.nasdaq.com/article/create-a-plan-for-a-meaningful-retirement-cm384893

www.huffingtonpost.com/arianna-huffington/its-time-to-retire-our-definition-of-retirement_b_5774878.html

www.nextavenue.org/10-keys-retirements-holy-grail/

www.nextavenue.org/10-tips-prepare-great-life-after-work/

www.forbes.com/sites/robertlaura/2012/10/31/how-to-find-your-passion-in-retirement/

www.wsj.com/articles/SB10001424127887323316804578163501792318298

Websites

www.encore.org/

www.vital-aging-network.org/

www.lifereimagined.aarp.org/

www.nextavenue.org/

www.findpurposeafterwork.com/

www.sage-ing.org/reading-list/

www.successfulretirementguide.wordpress.com/

ABOUT THE AUTHOR

Paul Wilkes lectures across the country about the role of religious belief in individual lives as well the place and impact of religion in public life. As a commentator on religious issues, he has appeared on all major television networks.

In *Due Season: A Catholic Life*, his autobiography, was chosen by *Publishers Weekly* as one of the year's 100 outstanding books. In a review, *PW* called *In Due Season* "an exquisite memoir that often reads like a novel." His book, *In Mysterious Ways: The Death and Life of a Parish Priest*, was a Book of the Month Club selection and won a Christopher Award. In addition to *Merton*, which aired on PBS, Paul was host, writer, and associate producer of the acclaimed television series, *Six American Families*, which won a DuPont-Columbia award for documentary excellence.

He has written for many national magazines, such as *The New Yorker, The Atlantic,* and *The New York Times Magazine,* and was a reporter for the *Baltimore Sun* and the *Boulder Daily Camera.* He served as an officer in the U.S. Navy.

He has been a visiting writer and guest lecturer at Clark University, Columbia University, the University of Pittsburgh, College of the Holy Cross, Boston University, and Brooklyn College. He was Welch Visiting Chair at the University of Notre Dame, and Distinguished Visiting Professor at the University of North Carolina at Wilmington.

Paul has been honored for his body of work with a Distinguished Alumnus Award from Columbia University's Graduate School of Journalism, where he received his advanced degree, and with a By-Line Award from Marquette University, where he graduated.

Paul lives in Wilmington, North Carolina, with his wife Tracy, who founded DREAMS, an arts program for at-risk children. The Wilkes have two grown sons, Noah and Daniel. In addition to Homes of Hope, Paul is a co-founder of CHIPS (Christian Help in Park Slope), a Brooklyn center that has served the poor and homeless young mothers and children for almost forty years.

OTHER BOOKS BY PAUL WILKES

Autobiography
In Due Season: A Catholic Life

Nonfiction
The Art of Confession: Renewing Yourself through the Practice of Honesty
Holding God in My Hands: Personal Encounters with the Divine
Beyond the Walls: Monastic Wisdom for Everyday Life
The Seven Secrets of Successful Catholics
The Good Enough Catholic: A Guide for the Perplexed
And They Shall Be My People: An American Rabbi and His Congregation
The Education of an Archbishop
In Mysterious Ways: The Death and Life of a Parish Priest
Merton: By Those Who Knew Him Best
Companions Along the Way
Six American Families
These Priests Stay
Trying Out the Dream: A Year in the Life of an American Family

Fiction
Temptations

For Children
Fitzgo, the Wild Dog of Central Park
My Book of Bedtime Prayers

Parish/Church Excellence
Excellent Catholic Parishes: The Guide to Best Places and Practices
Excellent Protestant Congregations: The Guide to Best Places and Practices
Best Practices from America's Best Churches